CUSTOMERS
DON'T BITE

CUSTOMERS DON'T BITE

Selling with Confidence

BY *Jules Steinberg*

FAIRCHILD PUBLICATIONS, INC.

NEW YORK

To my wife, Janet,
the object of
my most memorable sale

Contents

Preface

Anyone who has observed the typical retail salesman as he goes about his daily task of attempting to trade his product or service for the American consumer's cash or credit can appreciate how natural it was to title this book *Customers Don't Bite.*

Our hero, more often than not, behaves as if his prospective customer is interested less in pleasure and more in revenge whenever he enters the store. It would never do, some say, to approach the prospect too rapidly. In these days of cost-conscious management, when each salesman's moves are carefully plotted and his contribution to profit analyzed daily, it would be dating ourselves to suggest a time-consuming (no matter how small), polite inquiry if "we can be of service." Another school of practitioners of the art of salesmanship behaves as if only a clod, unschooled in contemporary sales psychology, would consider asking for an order before the customer has unmistakably signaled his intention to buy by demanding that he be sold.

In short, judging from the specimens that one encounters these days in almost any retail establishment, salesmen are required to deal with prospects at arm's length. Better yet, something more than arm's length would be advisable, because, or so it appears, customers are vicious and capable of biting the hand that serves them.

Of course one does, occasionally, run across the salesman who seems to delight in living dangerously. Depending upon his mood, this extremely extroverted individual may drop his reading when a prospect enters the store and even launch, uninvited, into a pitch that uses the term "the hottest thing since Coca-Cola," or some other shopworn comparison. He might pause long enough to permit a question or two. However, by the time he is ready to write the order, the customer had best be prepared to accept delivery at the time and date offered, or the salesman will turn, disdainfully, on his heels and head for a more lucrative conversation with his fellow employees at the water-cooler.

Fortunately for the nervous systems of those principally concerned—the prospect and the store's owner—this second type of sales personality doesn't seem to last long in one establishment. His ego cannot be contained in a place of business so unspeakably mismanaged and catering to a clientele consisting of such a shortsighted segment of the public that it fails to appreciate the tremendous values offered. Therefore, this individual usually falls prey to the flattering remarks of some wholesale supplier who convinces him that he has all the business acumen of an Andrew Carnegie, and that opening his own store (with that supplier's line, of course) is the first step on the road to creating another Sears Roebuck.

All of this leaves our timid hero of the first part in sole

and soulful possession of the sales floor. The fortunes of the over 1.5 million retail enterprises in this country, in the main, rise or fall on his ability to adjust to the daily confrontation of prospect and salesman. Whether he likes it or not, his shoulders bear the weight of moving some $145 billion of merchandise off retail sales floors and shelves into American homes each year. In this regard, he stands as the essential link between the public and the geniuses of big business who have dedicated themselves to an endless production of what the public—whether or not it knows it—really wants.

This book, then, is concerned less with "how to sell" than it is with a personality profile of both parties to the sales transaction. There can be no doubt that, once they get to know each other better, they will respect the motives that each brings to the drama unfolding, literally, millions of times each day on retail sales floors across the country.

Contrary to what many consumers suspect, the average salesman—if, indeed, one does exist—is not some untrained individual, unsuited for any other line of work. There are people in this selling game who sincerely feel that they are making a contribution, no matter how small, to the public's happiness. They equate their work with that of such other dispensers of comfort and tranquility as plumbers and psychiatrists, and their pay scale is approximately two-thirds of the former and one-fifth of the latter. In the following pages, we shall learn how this keystone of the American distribution system equips himself for his daily battle against the frustrations of sales quotas, overdrawn drawing accounts, and shoppers who are really relatives of the competition down the street "just making comparisons."

Hopefully, too, we will see that the American public

does not live in dollar bill-paneled houses adorned with lampshades made from the skins of salesmen who attempted to part them from their money. In fact, we may discover that people really do enjoy buying and that the true job of the retail salesman is to assist people in doing what they want to do. Yet, perhaps strangest of all to most salesmen who are genuinely trying to earn an honest living, especially those who sell nonessential products or services, will be the realization that customers don't bite.

JULES STEINBERG

October 1969
Chicago

CUSTOMERS
DON'T BITE

Chapter 1

Your Imagination Can Make or Break You

Too many years ago, a popular comedian left his mark upon the world of public entertainment with something called "droodles." These were simple sketches calculated to amuse and challenge the imagination of an audience. For example, he'd ask, "What's this?"

More than likely the humor is lost in the much faster pace of today's living, but it seemed very funny at the time to answer, "A man with a bow tie who got too close to an elevator door."

Got the stomach for another? If so, try this:

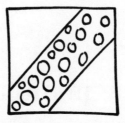

If you don't know that that's a giraffe passing a second-story window, you just aren't old enough to remember Roger Price and his daffy drawings. More to the point, you are missing out on an opportunity to exercise your imagination—one of the most essential tools for a good salesman and the one that is least used. If you don't believe it, try this one on your friends and business associates:

Most individuals will tell you that the above drawing is "a circle," "the sun," or "the moon," or some other obvious reference. A select few, with imaginations better than most, will reply that it is "a hole in a fence." These are people with the ability to see beyond their noses to the exciting world all around them. They can picture a poorly-dressed sales prospect buying an expensive piece of merchandise because they are trained to visualize the hole (solid circle) inside the fence (dotted line).

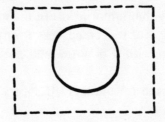

If you truly desire to be more than an ordinary sales-man—or, for that matter, more than an ordinary any-thing—you should perfect this ability. It's not difficult, and it can open an entirely new set of challenges and rewards to your physical and psychological talents.

Within the past quarter of a century, the medical pro-fession has grown to appreciate the role the imagination plays in keeping us physically well. The so-called "miracle cures" of apparently hopeless invalids are now recognized as being triumphs of the imaginative powers of the mind over the body, and numerous authoritative works attest to the fact that we can imagine ourselves in or out of very real painful situations.

During World War II, Dr. Henry K. Beecher of Harvard University compared the reactions to pain of 150 wounded soldiers on the Anzio beachhead battleground in Italy with those of a like number of male civilian surgical patients in the United States. "The striking thing about the war wounds, and the men involved," Dr. Beecher stated, "was their comparative freedom from pain." Only one-quarter of the entire group of badly wounded servicemen, when questioned seven to twelve hours after being wounded, had enough pain to want anything done about it. On the other hand, more than 80 percent of the civilian patients, when interviewed an average of less than four hours after sur-gery, had pain severe enough to request a narcotic.

Dr. Beecher concluded: "In a situation in which a wound has great advantage, and means escape from over-powering anxiety and fear of death on the battlefield (as in the case of war wounds terminating military service), extensive wounds are associated with comparatively little pain. In a situation where the wound connotes disaster (for example, major surgery in civil life), lesser wounds are associated with far more pain than in the former situation.

The essential difference appears to be the difference in anxiety level in the two cases, in the attitude of the patient, and in his reaction to his wound."*

An entirely new branch of "psychosomatic" medicine has evolved out of research such as this. However, the benefits of a mind trained to project itself into situations more conducive to individual happiness are hardly confined to physical matters. To a very large degree, a few simple exercises in perfecting your imagination will enable you to develop other talents that you may have possessed all of your life, but that have gone largely unutilized because of the distractions of modern civilization.

Naturally, it is foolish to expect that you can be an accomplished pianist, for example, if you cannot tell one musical note from another. On the other hand, it has been proven many times over that few of us operate on more than 30 percent of our potential ability, whether we are thinking in terms of playing a musical instrument, engaging in a sports event, or making a sale.

As indicated above, one of the inhibiting factors to our ability to function at full or even near-full potential is the complexity of twentieth-century life. For one thing, so many sights and sounds bombard our senses these days that it is virtually impossible for any particular one to truly and fully register.

You may have noticed how a concert lover attempts to overcome such intrusions on his evening's enjoyment by not only cupping his ears, but also closing his eyes—the better to *hear*. When one stops to think about it, it is not so strange that shutting off the sensations of sight should enhance one's ability to better concentrate on what he hears.

Childbirth With Hypnosis, William S. Kroger, M.D. and Jules Steinberg, Doubleday & Company, Inc., 1961.

Further evidence of this power of concentration to improve a certain ability can be observed in what people do in order to better see objects at a far distance—they squint! This act, shutting off peripheral distractions, actually improves one's eyesight. It's a simple experiment. Try it yourself, and see how much you can increase your power in this area.

If concentration works to improve the senses—and it does—it is even more effective in developing talents such as sales ability. Ideally, therefore, we should approach each work day with no thought of family problems, concern over health, or other nonbusiness considerations. Certainly, this is easier stated than done, yet you can vastly improve your sales performance if you will assign some hours after your working day is through to these other thoughts.

Such things as settling an argument with your wife or disciplining your children are important to your overall happiness, but permitting these thoughts to intrude on your working time is not only shortchanging your boss, it is seriously hampering your performance in all business and personal tasks. To better put everything into its proper perspective, you might try designating the hour between eight and nine P.M. as your "worry hour." Then you can fully concentrate on these other matters, and if one hour is not sufficient to handle all of your distractions, you can carry some thoughts over to tomorrow's worry period. You may even be surprised to discover that the very problem you have put off considering will have disappeared by the time its allotted worry period comes around.

Once you have mastered the ability to put every thought in its place, the better to concentrate on the task at hand, it is time to work on perfecting your imagination. "Work" is perhaps the wrong word to use here, because this can be a most rewarding and fun experience.

Just as, to a large extent, you are as healthy as you imagine yourself to be, you are as good a salesman as you think you are. If you still doubt the power of your mind to improve your talents in such matters, imagine yourself, for a moment, attempting to walk the length of a plank only one foot wide. If you think of the plank as lying on the ground, you will have little difficulty "seeing" yourself easily walking across. However, visualize the plank suspended many feet in the air, between two tall buildings, and notice how much trouble you have in "seeing" yourself safely across.

In the latter instance, obviously, your mind's eye pictures your body dashed on the pavement below. It is this horrible prospect, which your imagination sees all too clearly, that inhibits your chances of navigating the same board you could easily traverse if it were on the ground.

Applied to the sales situation, you can picture yourself as either a "supersalesman" or just another "order-taker." It is impossible to overemphasize the fact that, to a large extent, you will be the one you think you are.

Regrettably, few of us have had sufficient training in the uses of our imagination, and fewer still devote the necessary time each day to developing this part of our personality. Without regular practice, our imaginations soon wither and we become slaves to the pressures of everyday living. This need not be so. In fact, the biggest obstacle to the exercise of imagination is that the procedure is so easy most individuals either feel foolish following the brief but necessary routine or they refuse to believe that it will work.

You can begin your exercises in imagination by setting aside a specific period each day for practice. Optimistically, this will be twenty minutes to a half hour in the morning, before breakfast, and a similar length of time before the evening meal. The exact time you spend in practice will, of course, depend upon your routine and how serious you are about getting started on this new adventure.

Select some quiet room at home. If it's at all possible, choose a place free from family or any outside disturbance, such as a ringing telephone. After all, you won't be in this sanctum long enough to miss much in the way of important news.

Once you have chosen your "retreat" area, check to make certain that it contains a minimum of distracting objects. By all means, the television receiver, if there is one present, should be *off*. Actually, the only furniture that should predominate in this room is one comfortable chair in which you can "sink" while earth-shattering problems, and some not so earth-shattering, swirl around you. It is just as essential, though, that you do not make your brief escape so complete that you feel inclined to fall asleep. There is a fine line between eliminating distractions—the better to concentrate—and relaxing the mind and body so as to make sleep an overpowering impulse.

Well, assuming that you have your "think tank" well prepared, to what use shall it be put? You might plunge right in and spend the half hour or so telling yourself that you are the world's best salesman. Surprisingly enough, some good could come of that, but the results would be far less than you could realize through a more orderly procedure of developing your imagination, and a slower pace has a much more lasting effect.

It is best to start with some simple exercise in imagination, unrelated to your normal business activity, such as imagining that your right arm is getting heavy and tired. With both feet planted firmly on the floor, while you sit in your chair with your eyes closed and your arms resting comfortably on the arms of the chair, just tell yourself, slowly, over and over again: "My right arm is getting heavy and tired." Spend no more than a few minutes at each session forming the words in your mind, and actually try to imagine the prickly sensation, starting at your fingertips, that accompanies the heavy, tired arm.

After a little practice—from a few days to two weeks—you will discover that you can make your arm heavy just by sitting down, closing your eyes, and thinking of the sensation. To restore the natural feeling to your arm, you need only count slowly backwards from ten, telling yourself that all heaviness is gone from your arm. Then, after you reach "one," take several deep breaths and open your eyes. Now you are well on your way toward developing a highly trained imagination that can serve you in a number of different ways.

You might, for one thing, select a favorite color—let us suppose that it is blue—and, with your eyes closed (even this is not essential once you have achieved some proficiency in "imagineering"), tell yourself that when you think of blue your arm will get heavy. Conversely, when you think of red your arm will feel naturally light.

It honestly doesn't require much of an imagination to realize where you can go from here with this newly developed talent. A practiced person can use the thought of a favorite color, number, or what have you to better concentrate on a task at hand, restore a calm attitude in the midst of turmoil, feel less tired physically or emotionally, or even—after still longer periods of practice—virtually eliminate pain. However, our chief concern here is in the specific area of salesmanship, and it is to this subject that we should direct our refined sense of imagination.

Unfortunately, few of us start our adult lives with the thought that we want to be salesmen. At best, the majority see selling as a stepping-stone to some other position, such as manager or even owner of a business enterprise. Just because the number of such vacancies "at the top" are limited, this could lead to moments of frustration subconsciously taken out on some customer who has no way of knowing that, while serving her, we are merely biding our time until a better opportunity comes along.

Then, too, customers do have a way of bringing their own emotional problems, albeit unwittingly, into the store. Of course they do! They are subjected to the same stresses of contemporary living as the rest of us, suffer the same prejudices and frustrated ambitions; and so it should come as no surprise that the first person they meet—more often than not the first hapless salesman of the day—should bear the brunt of their hostilities.

It serves no useful purpose to say that this situation is unfair. That is the way our civilization is put together. Along with domestic quarrels, automobiles that won't start when you're already late for work, unreasonable traffic policemen, and a host of other irritations, they make up your sales day. The best way to cope with each of these is to "see" or imagine yourself safely through the situation. In plain words, think of your color blue and tell yourself that you will not be annoyed.

If you can picture yourself enjoying the sensation of writing the sales ticket for a particularly difficult customer, you are more than halfway through the sale. If you can see yourself as the unruffled, mild-mannered individual you can be, nothing need truly upset you. And, if your self-image is of one who accepts his lot in life with good grace, and of one who can imagine the exciting challenge inherent in almost any job, you will be happier at your work.

All it requires is patience, practice, and the realization that you are, more than likely, three times better than you think you are. Attempting to achieve true sales proficiency without these things is very much the same as riding a horse backwards. You may get where you intended to go, but the ride will, at best, be unsafe and bumpy, and the view will be less than appealing.

Chapter 2

Salesmen Can't Afford to Forget

Is there anything more important to the success of a salesman than a good memory? If there is, we've already forgotten about it—which serves to reinforce the notion that, as a tool for converting sales prospects into buyers, memory has few equals.

A salesman who reads product features to a shopper, or even one who refers to notes, is little better than a mail-order catalogue on two feet. In fact, he's worse, because the act of reading from a fancy point-of-purchase display piece not only betrays a lack of knowledge on the part of the salesman, but is also insulting to the prospect. None of us like to be given the impression that we are so lacking in education that we cannot read for ourselves. Furthermore, if this were all we expected from a salesperson, we wouldn't have bothered to leave our "typical" home, which is probably sagging under the weight of the direct-mail solicitations so representative of today's American sales effort.

Then, too, being only human, potential customers like to feel that they spend their time only with "important" people. This gives the well-dressed salesman an initial advantage, especially if, in wearing a flower in the button-hole of his suit jacket, he gives the impression of being some sort of manager. Think of how much further this advantage can be exploited if, in addition, he greets the customer by name!

"I, myself, must be somebody special," the prospect will tell himself. "This sales executive, who meets so many people in the course of a business day, has taken the trouble to remember my name. The very least I can do, in return, is to listen to his sales story."

Whether your prospects are that articulate, even in talking to themselves, or whether they only go so far as thinking of you as a "nice guy," the result is the same—a more attentive audience. And that is as good a start as any salesman has the right to expect.

The entire list of benefits to be derived from having a good memory is practically endless. In addition to the two "pluses" already cited, it could include such things as not missing appointments, recalling telephone numbers, or even remembering to keep the stock dusted and in place after the manager has mentioned it once, to say nothing of bringing to mind the name of a prospect who inquired some time ago about a piece of merchandise that just arrived today.

With all of this "going for it," why, you might well ask, doesn't more formal memory-training occupy the attention of those engaged in sales? Perhaps the answer lies in the fact that memory, as in the case of imagination, is something which we use more or less every day. This very familiarity makes it easy for us to fancy ourselves beyond the need for education and practice in the art. Yet there isn't a single individual who could not immediately benefit from a better understanding of the subject.

From the strictly scientific point of view, "memory" has some very interesting aspects, which, if properly appreciated, can immeasurably increase our efficiency in this region of human activity. Psychologists, who specialize more in researching the causes of such phenomena than in their application to everyday living, tell us, for example, that there are three clearly definable steps to the process of memorizing. In scholarly circles, these are referred to as "learning," "retention," and "recall." To put it another way, before we can even begin to draw upon our memory (recall), we must, first of all, have bothered to learn the subject (learning) and have established some system for storing this information (retention) in our minds.

Contrary to what one might expect, these steps are just as easily taken as they are said. Indeed, when one thinks about the number of tasks we perform many times each day, "by heart" so to speak, such as picking up the correct eating utensil at mealtimes or crossing the street, which were once more or less painstakingly committed to memory but which are now performed without a second thought, we can appreciate how miraculously simple this procedure must be. It matters not that these essentially bodily movements are commonly referred to as "habits"— they all can be broken down into the three basic steps of learning, retention, and recall. It is to these areas that we must address ourselves if we are to make new, profitable "habits" out of the multitude of actions that make up the present, hectic world of business.

One of the earliest pioneers in the field of memory research was the nineteenth-century German psychologist Hermann Ebbinghaus. It was he who first formulated the theory that a good portion of what we forget was never correctly learned in the first place. Using himself as his principal experimental subject, Ebbinghaus developed his well-known "curve of learning," which indicates that over 75 percent of what has been learned is forgotten within twenty-four hours of the start of memorization, but that the remaining impressions last for comparatively long periods of time. The memory-loss rate for those retained facts and impressions is so low that many of those mental images remain with us for a lifetime.

Such research has conclusively proven that numerous and varied subconscious factors—i.e., the true depth of our desire to learn, our emotions at the time of attempted memorization, etc.—either aid or impede the original learning process. The reader is undoubtedly familiar with the "conditioning" experiments of the Russian psychologist I. P. Pavlov. In these, using food for hungry dogs as the stimulus for learning, the experimenter taught animals to respond to the sound of a bell. These lessons were "learned" so well that the ringing of the bell, even though no food was present, was sufficient to cause activity in the salivary glands of the animals. At this point it would be rhetorical to ask whether such tests did not also demonstrate some reason for the fact that a "hungry" salesman seems to learn his business lessons—representing, in the long run, food on the table—better than his more comfortable contemporaries.

All of this is not meant to imply that one must remain in a constant state of undernourishment to improve his memory. On the contrary, the distraction of an empty, growling stomach can effectively prevent learning many things that might prove useful after the hunger pains have passed. On the other hand, the correct inference from these observations is that nothing can be learned unless the proper stimulus is present, and unlearned subject matter cannot be committed to memory.

Do you, for instance, know the license-plate numbers on your automobile? If you do, you are representative of a minority of car owners, the majority of whom, when they need their license numbers, càn either look at the car or refer to their registrations. Why, then, bother to memorize the series? Your telephone number, however, is another matter. Almost as soon as the phone was installed you memorized the number, because it would prove to be embarrassing and difficult to look up when you needed it.

It is just as true that you will not remember a name, face, or product feature unless you consider it important enough to learn in the first place. Later in this chapter we will explore some simple methods for remembering such things, but these procedures are all based on improving your ability to recall. They cannot draw from your mind something that is not there. Properly motivating yourself to learn, with some physical or psychological reward such as a new car you will buy with this year's sales commissions, or the pleasure of seeing your name at the head of this week's sales performance list, will automatically improve your memory by a minimum of 25 percent.

At this point, the less said about the retention aspect of memory the better. Certainly, the subject is important. Without the ability to store information learned, our minds would be much like sieves, and data would never be on hand for "recall" when it was needed. However, the little that is known about how the human brain actually files the hundreds of millions of bits of information upon which it must constantly draw is useful only for discussion in a medical text. Far more fruitful research has been done in the areas of getting learned messages to the brain—along "sensory" nerves located near the surface of the skin (touch), eyes (sight), ears (sound), nose (smell), and mouth (taste)—and from the brain along outgoing, or "motor," nerve paths. It is along these latter circuits, which motivate such actions of ours as walking and speaking, that the recalled information will travel.

For centuries, man has been preoccupied with programs for improving his powers of recall—or at least making it appear as if his memory is much better than it really is. Some of these schemes, while hardly scientific, are quite ingenious. For example, when Franklin D. Roosevelt was President of the United States, he adopted a rather unique method for working himself out of situations in which he forgot the name of an individual he had met before.

"I'm terribly sorry," the President would confess, "but I've forgotten your name."

"Why, it's Smith, Mr. President," the caller might reply.

"Of course, Mr. Smith, I knew that, but I meant your given name," was FDR's prompt rejoinder.

Although such tricks may relieve the pressure on one's memory, they can and often do prove to be most embarrassing. For instance, there is the classic case of the individual who, upon meeting someone whose name he knew he should know, would ask for a spelling of the name, and be icily told, "J-O-N-E-S."

Practically all bona fide attempts at memory improvement involve some sort of association. Any schoolboy who ever tied a string around his finger to remind him of some task to be performed knows that. For those readers too old to recall their school days, the object here was to tie the string in some easily spotted place, so that it could not be forgotten. Then, when the boy looked at the string, he would remember what it was he had to do. All things considered, this method of recall still works fairly well—for schoolboys.

However, it would be somewhat distracting for all concerned in a sales transaction for the salesman to walk around with numerous strings tied to his fingers. Furthermore, as we are about to learn, undirected association can prove to be as troublesome as forgetting completely. A case in point would be the salesman who wished to remember the name of an overweight customer named Gross. One look at his customer's stomach convinced this salesman that he had a perfect association. From now on, it would be "stomach" to "large" to "Gross," or so the salesman thought.

At his very next meeting with Mr. Gross, our hero took one look at the buyer's waistline and promptly addressed him as "Mr. Lodge." A perfectly understandable mistake under the circumstances, but one that would not have occurred had the salesman learned the most important rule about using association as an aid to recall.

Logical associations will not work! This point cannot be overemphasized. In fact, the more illogical the association you make with anything you are trying to recall, the better will be your chances of correctly remembering it. Here's a good place to put to work that newly found imagination of yours, which you learned to perfect during your reading of the preceding chapter. Don't be afraid to let yourself go! Start right now by thinking of something you wish to remember and associating it with the most ridiculous thing (noun) you can think of. You don't have to be afraid of this one, because no one will ever know the association you are making. It will be something strictly between you and your much-improved power of recall.

Merely making some far-fetched connection, though, will not be enough, especially if you stop at the mere thought of the connecting word. You must actually *see* the association in your mind's eye. This means precisely what you think it does. Connect the words—the one you wish to remember and the association one—with some sort of action in your imagination. If Mr. Gross were your customer, and you decided to remember his name by associating his name with a gross of boxes, *see* Mr. Gross sitting atop those boxes piled high on the floor. Remember, too, that there are no censors in your mind. Make whatever wild association comes to your mind. It makes as much recall sense to connect the initials W.C. with a water closet as it does to associate A.C. with a highly-charged individual.

Of course, you'll want to put first things first. Remember that you won't be able to recall any name unless, to begin with, you learned it. This may mean asking for it, if it is not volunteered. If you are not certain as to the spelling, inquire about it. Most people will be flattered by your interest. You can also assist the learning process, if you will form the habit of repeating the name as often as you can in the conversation. All this while, of course, you will be looking for a distinguishing feature in the individual and forming a *ridiculous* association between that feature and the person's name.

You'll be amazed to discover how easy and natural this entire process becomes with just a little practice. That, plus these few simple rules, will vastly improve your ability to recall names:

1. Make certain that you hear the name. Unless the spelling is so simple that the question seems ridiculous, it is a good idea to ask how it is spelled.
2. Use the name as often as you can in your conversation.
3. Seek out some distinguishing feature in the individual whose name you wish to remember.

4. Form the most outlandish association you can think of between that feature and the person's name. Don't forget to *see* the picture of the association in your mind.

As stated above, this entire business of recall works best when you devote some time to practicing the art. Just for a starter, consider a day during which you have encountered eight sales prospects, each of whose names you wish to remember so that, at your next call, you can get off to a better start by greeting them by name. On this day, we shall meet:

Mr. Goodwin—an average sort of fellow, in his forties, with no particular distinguishing features except a rather long, pointed nose.

Let's start right in by associating Mr. Goodwin with that nose. Form any mental image that you wish. We might suggest picturing Mr. Goodwin in a horse race making a "good win" by the length of his nose, but, remember, you are the one who will have to recall his name, so form a mind picture with which you will be comfortable.

Mr. Blank—take away his mustache, and this gentleman would look just about like any other.

Surely, you can form your own association for this one!

Mrs. Grabowski—a rather plump woman with a pleasant personality and a fairly attractive face, except for a mole on her right cheek.

To recall this one, we could picture the customer grabbing some merchandise, while we shouted "ow," and then fleeing the scene on skis.

Mac—sorry, that's all this fellow would tell us when we asked for his name. As a matter of fact, his full, bushy beard marks him as an individualist, and if he wants to be called "Mac" the next time we meet, we'll oblige him by associating that name with his beard.

Mr. Ziesler—also a very nice chap, and one who is, potentially, a good customer. We won't want to speak aloud about his baldness, but we will want to use that fact to recall his name. By the way, that's pronounced: "zees-ler."

Can you see this customer swimming in high seas, trying to catch a woman (her) while his bald head is the only visible thing above the surface of the water?

Mrs. Graham—too bad that this customer is so overweight. (Perhaps she's eaten too many graham crackers.)

Here's another connection you can probably make without too much difficulty.

Julie—one more individualist who replies with just her first name. We don't mind, though. We're busy making a connection between her name and the dimple in her cheek.

Mr. Johnston—unfortunately, this gentleman walks with a most pronounced limp. However, we'll use that observation and the fact that we hear his name as "John-stone" the better to form an association to assist us in recalling that name.

The relationship between a stone tied to that leg, causing the limp, is fairly obvious. We'll leave it to your imagination to connect the "John" to the rest of the picture.

Okay, now let's see how well you've done. With the images you've formed clearly set in your mind, and without reviewing what you've just read, read the list of features below and try to relate each to a customer's name. Don't try too hard, and don't worry if you miss a few. With a little practice in imagination and image-forming, you'll soon be batting 1.000. Here we go. What's the name of the customer whose most distinguishing feature is:

Mustache?
Overweight?
Long nose?

Beard?
Mole?
Dimple?
Limp?
Bald?

The more you exercise your imagination the easier it will be for you to improve your memory. Of course, you don't have to and shouldn't confine yourself to recalling names. Another area in which you will find your much-improved memory useful is in remembering product features without the aid of any written reference. Even with the multitude of models and features on today's products, you should have little difficulty in recalling details of the entire line.

The method you will use in this project is exactly the same as the principal of association you used to fix the names of your customers and/or prospects in your mind. That is, the most ridiculous mind-picture you can conjure up involving the feature you wish to remember. Naturally, to keep your images in their proper file, you will also want to tie in the product itself to the scene.

For example, suppose you wished to remember the razor-sharp feature of your item. You might picture the product, no matter how big it is, standing on edge and cutting a clean, deep line in the floor. Applying the rules of association that you have already learned, you can readily realize that this "scene" could work for anything except a linoleum-cutting device. This is true because the image is too logical for that particular instrument. It would be just as inadequate for any knifelike item. To recall the keen-edge feature of any of these, we could form the picture of a man shaving with it.

In our sales pitches, too, it is often useful to remember not only all of the product's features, but the order in which these should be presented to a prospective buyer. Sometimes this order is so apparent that little if any memorization is required. At other times, though, we must employ some sort of continuous-form memory system so that not a single important product feature will be overlooked.

If, for instance, your item is not only razor sharp but also folds into one's pocket, you could imagine a miniature man shaving while in a folded position in someone's pocket. As silly as that might seem, it's safe to say that you won't forget the picture for a long while. As a matter of fact, providing you use it from time to time in relating your sales message, there is no reason for you ever to forget it.

This continuous-form type of remembering could go on indefinitely, from one feature to another. All that is required is fitting one image into the next. To see how this would work in an actual sales situation, let us imagine, to begin with, that you have just been employed in a sales capacity by the Widget Manufacturing Company. The principal features of the product, which you must "pitch" to a prospective customer within the next half hour, are its large capacity, sturdy construction, availability in choice of bright colors, heavy duty motor, wheels to make the unit portable, simplicity of operation, low operating costs, five-year guarantee on the motor, and two-year guarantee on all other parts.

To fix these features quickly and permanently and in order in your mind, you will, naturally, start with the large capacity of your widget. Can you "see" it floating gently on an ocean of water, and loaded to capacity with a crowd of people? If so, or if you have formed an equally outlandish association picture in your mind, you are well on your way to learning your sales lesson in time to make that sale.

Now imagine, if you will, your floating, loaded widget being nudged by sharks who, because of the sturdy construction of the unit, are unable to harm the people inside. A good, illogical connection, but remember that one of your own choosing will do just as well.

Our sharks, though, are not colored the traditional gray. Indeed, there is a wide assortment of bright colors represented in the school surrounding our sturdily constructed widget, loaded with people and floating serenely on the sea. Do you still have the picture in your mind? Good, then let's continue.

Our fish are truly strange. Each is powered by a heavy-duty motor strapped to its back. Laugh, if you will. In fact, a smile on your face right now is a good sign that the associations we are making are really "way out." You can't help remembering those heavy-duty motors on the brightly colored sharks, which are nudging the sturdily constructed, large capacity widgets.

To continue: the motors on the backs of our fishes are all mounted on wheels so that they glide easily back and forth atop each shark. That's really as "sensible" as we dare get in our associations. Therefore, in forming your own image, start from here and let yourself go! Don't be afraid. We won't tell what you're thinking, if you don't. All your customer will hear will be a clear, logical story of the advantages of the product, culminating at this point with the fact that it can be conveniently moved about.

As we see them, the wheels on our motors each have two conspicuous buttons—one marked "on," the other "off." Mentally observe for yourself how simple it is to operate this widget. And, while you're about it, go back and try to recall the second mentioned feature of our product. Right! It was "sturdy construction," so let's proceed.

Our operating buttons are each fitted with a coin-holding device very much like a parking meter. However, unlike many other meters, these accept only pennies—bringing to mind, of course, the low operating costs of our product. Can you picture yourself inserting a penny into one of those meters?

Good, because your pennies are most unusual, in that each has a big "5" stamped on its face. By now, it should not be difficult for you to see that that "5" represents the five-year guarantee on the motor. We've come a long way in a short time from our floating widget, but note the logical sequence to our illogical associations. Once you have that order fixed in your mind, you can't fail to remember any list—even if there are dozens of memory points involved.

Finally, we see that our hand, in the act of inserting a penny marked with a big "5" in the meter, passes over the body of the shark. Here, we can't help but note that there is a large "2" stenciled on the side of each fish. You're right! This stands for the two-year guarantee on all parts except the motor.

"All of this is very good," you might say, "if I were carrying a line of widgets. However, we haven't had a call for one of those in many a year. What do I do about remembering all of the features on each item in my present product mix?"

The question, of course, is in order. There's very little market for "memory experts" these days—unless, that is, you have a desire to parade your new talent at the next party you attend. For a real dollar-and-cents application of these recall techniques, you'll have to take each product in your line, and:

1. List its features in the order you would present them to a prospective buyer. Try, very hard, to find just one word that describes the point you wish to make, but make certain that it covers the subject and is as unlike any other word in your list as possible.

2. Start with the first descriptive-feature word and form some illogical association between that word and the product. Remember, you can't get too far out on this one.

3. Now, starting with that first association, merge each new feature word into your mind-picture. Take them in order, but from that point on remove all restrictions on your imagination. Then sit back and permit the list of features to roll easily from your tongue, like the professional salesman you are.

One more test, before leaving you to your good memory:

How about our widget salesman? Without turning back in your reading, can you recite his list of product features? We'll give you a hint. Start with a floating, loaded widget. What does that bring to mind? Now, proceed to sharks trying to dent the widget, and go on to colorful fish. What does each have on its back? On what are these mounted? How do we start the fish moving? What coin does the device take? What number is marked on the side of the coin and what number is stenciled on the side of the fish?

See how easy it is? Now all you have to do is find somebody who might be in the market for a widget. Failing that, apply the principals you have learned to whatever it is you are selling, and watch your sales curve climb.

Chapter 3

The Near-Lost
Art of Listening

In His infinite wisdom, it has been said, the good Lord gave man two ears and one mouth. However, with his insatiable vanity, man seems determined to compensate for this trick of nature by using the latter twice as much as the former. What a pity!

Too many of us, it seems, go through life spending so much time talking about what we know that we leave hardly any time for listening and learning. It is almost as if we're so afraid of being alone—of losing a prospect—that we don't dare shut our mouths because, once he has the floor, the other fellow might say no. This hallmark of twentieth-century man is not confined to salesmen, of course, except that, to a great degree, we are all—every one of us—always "pitching."

Listen! A rare but truly rewarding experience awaits the person who will pause to count the minutes in a day when his eardrums are not being assaulted by one human-created sound or another. If nothing else, his own silence will contribute to the general welfare, and give his friends something to think about other than their own troubles.

"Something wrong?" they'll eventually ask.

"No, why?"

"Well, you're so . . . so . . . so quiet."

"I'm just listening."

And, because the situation is so unusual, they'll probably reply: "All right. If you don't want to tell me . . ."

Yet, as every good salesman knows, the principal distinguishing feature between a professional and an amateur in this business is the ability of the "pro" to resist the temptation to fall in love with the sound of his own voice. His are the sales that are made with such apparent ease and little fanfare that it almost seems as if the buyer has talked himself into the transaction. Indeed, this is most often the case, because as we shall learn in the next chapter, a successful sale hinges to a great degree on the seller catering to the buyer's needs. Surely, the best if not the only way to find out what the other fellow wants, and registering this with what we have to offer, is to listen intelligently.

S. I. Hayakawa, the best-known of our contemporary semanticists (one who studies language as an integral part of the art of communicating) reminds us that this is much easier said than done. Although the first way to discover another's thoughts or point of view is to listen to him, Hayakawa says, the training of most ververbalized professional intellectuals (naturally, this would encompass most salesmen) is in the opposite direction. To listen effectively, we must see the problem the way the speaker sees it, he adds. This means not so much sympathy, which is feeling for the other individual, but empathy, which is experiencing with him. It follows, therefore, that a good listener is one who can imagine or "see" himself in the other's shoes—a difficult task, as most of us who stop to think about it will agree.

It is small wonder, though, that most of us find this a

difficult lesson to learn. We just can't help talking. Almost from the day we are born, we are taught that "the squeaking wheel gets the most grease." Stand at the nursery window in almost any hospital maternity ward and observe how much attention the squawking baby gets while his quieter contemporaries receive scant notice from the staff. And isn't this learning experience bolstered by the modern "demand" method of feeding when the parents take the infant home?

In any case, the habit of *not* listening is started and reinforced in our childhood. Unfortunately, many adults never learn better. We are all painfully familiar with the grown-up child, sometimes a buyer and sometimes a seller, who still communicates by crying and whining. For better or worse, there always seems to be someone around ready to interpret the cries and comfort the "infant." The wonder, then, is not why these individuals behave as they do, but rather why more of us do not foresake the give and take of talking and listening to rely instead upon screaming our demands at one another.

Until the recent introduction of "listening" courses at some universities, there was, literally, no opportunity for a businessman or any other student of human relations to improve his skill in this important art. It was Dr. Paul Rankin of Ohio State University who, after keeping a log on the activities of sixty-five white collar workers over a period of several months, alerted the academic world to the problem. Over 70 percent of our waking hours are spent in some form of verbal communication, Dr. Rankin determined. The greatest share of this time (45 percent) is spent listening, while 30 percent is reserved for speaking, 16 percent for reading, and the remaining 9 percent for writing. Think of it! We spend more moments in a day listening than doing anything else. Yet most of us have had far more formal training in the less important forms of communication.

Fortunately, you don't have to return to college to improve your listening skills. As in the case of so many other things we have to do to live a happier, more fruitful life, it's all a matter of exercising your imagination and powers of concentration—two talents most conducive to a "full" life about which you, hopefully, learned much in Chapter 1, and which you applied, in Chapter 2, to improve your memory. Now it's time to direct these same lively arts to the three things for which you must "listen" most—silence, signs, and sounds.

Perhaps because it is so little used, silence in itself is a truly underrated form of communication. As we noted earlier, the person who suddenly falls silent is often suspected of being either physically ill or emotionally upset. In fact, the old joke about the individual who lived alongside a railroad track along which a train passed at the same time each day and who, when the train failed to arrive one day, said, "What's that?" unfortunately contains more truth than humor. We are so accustomed to sound that, when it is absent, we tend to assume that something is wrong. This is especially apparent in the case of the salesman, more often than not a neophyte, who is prone to interpret silence from a prospect as disapproval. Naturally, any party to a conversation who remains silent is communicating, too, but if you're doing the talking, why assume the worst instead of taking time out to listen for the real message?

The difficulty arises, in part, from the fact that a good salesman is expected to be enthusiastic about his product and completely familiar with all of its features. Our image of the all-American "pro" on the sales floor is one of a man with just one thought in mind—make that sale! We are, disturbingly, less "at home" with the equally accurate

picture of the average prospect for whom buying is just
one activity in an otherwise crowded day. Surely, it is better
logic to assume that this person has less knowledge than
you about your product. (And thank goodness for that! If
prospects knew everything, there'd be no need for salesmen.) We also can't expect this individual to match your
enthusiasm for whatever it is you're selling—at least not
until he's heard your story. His silence, therefore, may be
another way of saying: "Go ahead. I'm listening." If you
don't pause occasionally, you may miss the message.

Of course, there are times when silence should be a
warning signal to the salesman. We've all had the experience, at one time or another, of "pitching" to a prospect
who just stands there and says nothing, no matter what
we say, or how silent we ourselves become. Can anything
be more exasperating? Suggestions for meeting this kind
of "objection," with particular emphasis on not losing our
tempers, will be discussed in a subsequent chapter. We
mention it at this point only to note that silence can certainly be a sign that we have failed to strike a responsive
chord in the prospect, and that another direction of "attack" is indicated.

The one thing knowledgeable salesmen dread most
about silence is that it might mask some objection that the
prospect doesn't want to voice. (It is particularly difficult
to meet an objection when you don't know that it exists.)
A man purchasing an undergarment as a gift for his wife,
for example, might quite possibly find it difficult to say
that the size offered is too small—or too large—depending
upon one's cultural background. For this reason, it would
be a good idea to review your sales message, now, with
the object of ferreting out words and symbols that might
prove to be embarrassing to a prospect. Maybe you can't
eliminate them because they are too vital to your overall

sales story, but, knowing that they're there, you'll be better prepared to meet the moment of silence when it comes.

Pause frequently in your sales presentation, and give this silence a chance to be "heard." Perhaps it will be some objection that your prospective customer "feels," but that he doesn't quite know how to put into words. At other times, it may be something he thinks is too foolish to speak about, but that is important enough, to him, to spoil your sale. Unfortunately, these nonverbal objections are, at best, extremely difficult to "hear." However, your own silence, no matter how momentary, will give you the opportunity to observe certain telltale signs—the next dividend of intelligent listening.   *79 - 13119*

Behold the power of a physician's eyebrow! Even the strongest and healthiest patient will suffer some pangs of anxiety when, with his stethoscope to the patient's chest, the doctor simply raises that eyebrow. *Not a word need pass between them.* The patient may be getting a completely false message and need some reassurance, but there is no doubt that the simple sign established some sort of communication.

Also, in the sometimes equally serious and very important world of politics, we can see how signs do play a significant communicative role. Over the centuries, millions of men have fought and died for flags and other symbols. And who can forget how, in this generation, Great Britain's Winston Churchill, renowned orator that he was, rallied the free world behind, not a speech, but a simple gesture of two fingers raised in a sign for victory.

Although the signs a prospect makes, consciously or otherwise, during a presentation are not nearly as vital to the individual or to the group as those symbols just noted, they can be of great value to the salesman who "listens" for them.

Consider, for a moment, something you should be looking at anyway, the prospect's eyes. Is he looking back at you, or is he staring down at the floor or out the window? From your point of view, if you're pitching a product, the item itself, or at least an illustration, will serve as a focus of attention for those eyes. (A service sale is only slightly different in this regard, because a competent salesman can still draw the senses to something illustrating the benefits of that service.) The main point is that successful sales are as much the result of the prospect's concentration as the salesman's.

Naturally, you can do less about getting a prospect to concentrate than you can about applying yourself to the sale. Yet the task is far from hopeless, provided you remember that occasional pause in your talk to "listen" or "observe" just what the prospect is doing. If, indeed, you should discover that his eyes (and mind) are wandering, you can bring them back to where you want them simply by tapping the object with a pen or pencil. Surely you'll never wish to do this in anger—merely to emphasize a point—but the result is bound to be a much more attentive audience.

Another sign for which you should be alert is the position of the prospect's hands during the sale. (Among other things, if you're engaged in retail selling this can be rewarding in reducing losses through shoplifting, but in this case we're referring to movements of a different sort.) Have you ever noticed how imitative people are in their physical reactions? If just one individual coughs in a crowded theater, a ripple of coughing or throat clearing runs quickly through the group. A similar response occurs when a person in our crowd yawns. In that case, don't we all have to make an effort to suppress a yawn, too? Although this phenomenon has never been completely explained, psychologists and other behavioral scientists have dubbed it a manifestation of "ideomotor" reaction. Our concern, naturally, is less with the name and more with its application to successful salesmanship.

Using the principle of "ideomotor" reaction—or, if you prefer, "monkey see, monkey do"—you can direct the position of your prospect's hands easier than you can get him to follow the movement of your eyes.

Suppose that there is something pleasant to the touch—a smooth wood finish, a velvet-like fabric, etc.—about your product that is one of its sales features. Of course, you can invite the prospective buyer to enjoy the touch sensation, but how about the prospect who just doesn't want to get that involved? If the item you're selling is large enough to accommodate two hands without any embarrassment, you can get your shopper to feel it simply by doing so yourself. Many a customer has "sold himself" by touching buttons, twisting knobs, etc., after he, subconsciously, got the okay to do so by observing the salesman in action.

Naturally, to you the most important result of concentrating on listening will be a better ability to hear what your prospect is saying—or, to be more exact, the sounds he is making. What we call "language" is, after all, merely common agreement on the meaning of certain sounds. As we shall soon discover, the sounds that an individual makes are far more important than what he "says."

In searching for an example, the writer is reminded of a personal experience that occurred in Paris, France, during a business conference he was scheduled to address. Upon arriving at the meeting hall, we discovered that we had left our ticket of admission back at the hotel. It did little good to explain our plight to the guard, because he spoke only French and our command of that language was inadequate for the occasion. Undaunted, we squared our shoulders, threw our head back haughtily, and, waving a finger under the guard's nose, authoritatively shouted: "See here, my good man, there'll be no smoking in the auditorium." Then, we strode past the guardian at the door, just as if we had every right in the world to be there. It was, of course, not what we said, but *how* we said it that made the difference.

This bit of insight is hardly original. Anthropologists agree that, of the 25 or 30 million years during which man has inhabited the earth, less than half of that time has been spent in communicating via some formal language. Originally, together with other primates, man expressed his emotions and desires solely through a series of cries, grunts, moans, and shouts, which still make up a good part of what passes for conversation. Listen, and you will hear them!

It is extremely important for the salesman to appreciate the fact that the transition from communicating via sounds to "language" is far from complete. Nor has the development been uniformly the same for everyone. And, just to further complicate the meaning of sounds, each of us has an emotional level beyond which the veneer of civilization slips away and we substitute sounds for culturally learned words.

In theatrical circles, they tell the story of the great John Barrymore, who was touring the midwestern states with a road company of a Broadway show. Just before one performance, a bit-part actor got drunk, and the show's producer searched the town for someone with acting experience to take that small role. As luck would have it, the only qualified person was the local minister, who readily agreed to help out.

"It's quite easy, Reverend," the producer explained. "All you have to do is stand on the stage, and, at a certain point in the play, Mr. Barrymore will point a blank pistol at you and fire. Then you clutch at your heart, say, 'My God, I've been shot,' and fall to the floor. Think you can do it?"

"Oh, yes," the minister said. "There's just one thing. Because so many of my congregants will be in the audience, and they may not appreciate my taking the Lord's name in vain, I'd like to change that line to 'my goodness, I've been shot.'"

Somewhat reluctantly, everyone agreed, and the night of the performance they were in position on stage. The only small problem was that the producer forgot to tell the minister that, to add a bit of realism to the scene, a small cherry had been loaded down the barrel of the pistol. Well, the gun went off on schedule. The minister, good trouper that he was, put his hands to his heart, and said, "My goodness, I've been shot." However, as he started to slump to the floor, he noticed the growing patch of red on his chest and shouted, "God damn it! I have been shot!"

Each of us has such a "my goodness/God damn it" threshold. And because it will vary from one person to the next, the professional salesman is always on the alert for it. He will accept the fact that the same words hardly ever mean the same to two prospects, so he will "listen" both for the context of what's being said and for the mood of the other party. However, the problem of misunderstanding or misinterpreting another's remarks is not confined to emotional situations, nor even to the obvious differences in language. It is amazing, though, how many people, impressed more with sound than silence, will attempt to overcome the language barrier by shouting at a foreigner when listening for signs and sounds can be so much more effective.

When we speak the same tongue, the difficulties into which we get ourselves by not listening are even more pitiful. Our own American culture or environment has so many subcultures—based upon race, national origin, religion, age, etc., each with its own peculiar variations on the one language—that one sometimes gets the impression that he is traveling in a foreign land without leaving his neighborhood. Gone are the days when we can use or hear such words as "square"—does it mean "all right" or "on the level" or does it mean "out of tune with the times?"—and be certain of their meaning. Similarly, sales run "by popular demand," which once meant "more customers than could be satisfied the first time around," have now taken on the connotation of "the boss is still stuck with some of this merchandise and it must be moved at all costs."

It is even impossible to fall back upon the technical dictionary definition of words. There is little if any difference, we are told, between the "warranty" and "guarantee" on a product. If indeed there is none, why use them except to confuse the other fellow who may not be listening? To accent the obstacles we deliberately put in the path of understanding each other, an advertising agency in this country recently assembled all of the words we use to mean "group" as applied to different birds and animals. The reader may find even a partial listing of these group words illuminating.

A group of foxes, for example, is known as a "skulk." Many horses are a "field," while several finches are a "charm." Quite a few toads are a "knot," and a host of gulls is a "colony." Many cats are a "cluster," but a bunch of kittens are a "kindle." And if you happen to have several leopards about, you have a "leap," but a group of lions is a "pride."

"How did our language ever get into such a mess?" you might ask. "Is it any wonder that we have so much difficulty in speaking with each other?" These pertinent questions are, for the moment, best left to the anthropologists and semanticists who are making valiant efforts to find the answers. Perhaps the most fascinating of their findings so far is the fact that one of the most common mistakes made in verbal communication is the failure of people to "weigh" or take into account the classification into which the speaker falls. The absurdity of a salesman attempting to impugn the reputation of his competition by saying, "oh well, we all know that all salesmen lie," may be apparent here, but it passes, unchallenged, many times in conversation.

It is obvious, therefore, that, rather than attempting to reform our admittedly imperfect language, the reader who is more concerned with the end result of the communicative process is best advised to improve his listening skills. Although we have already indicated that this is simply a matter of concentrating on what's being said and how the speaker is behaving, there are some very definite impediments to listening with ease.

The first of these is our sometimes inability to be truly interested in what the other party is saying. Customers, even as the rest of us, can sometimes be bores. They will insist upon talking politics, sports, or about their own health—all of which can be useful clues to an alert salesman, but which can be equally distracting to the individual who has little true interest in them, and who has not trained himself to listen effectively. It is easy to "tune ourselves out" when we're there to talk about a sale and they persist in speaking of the weather. We may stand there politely, but are we listening or thinking about what we will say next?

Putting aside the distractions of even your own thoughts is not difficult if you will apply the lessons already learned. Further, it can help, if you will apply your imagination to "see" or visualize the prospect telling you that your pants are on fire or your place of business is burning down. You'd listen then, wouldn't you? Well, each time a potential customer takes his time to talk with you, no matter what he's saying, he is sending you a message vital to your security and future.

Another bad listening habit of which we are all more or less guilty is that of permitting ourselves to be "taken in" by emotionally laden words. Let's face it! None of us is so free of prejudice and fear that certain words cannot, to quote the current vernacular, "turn us on." It is impossible to present a list of such words, because they will vary from one individual to the next. For an Italian it may be "wop," for a Negro or black man it would, very likely, be "nigger," for a Jew it probably would be "kike," etc.

Successful human relations, and that of course includes selling anything, depends to a large measure upon our understanding that some people—often without meaning to be offensive—do use those words. It is a sad commentary on our society that, in some quarters, this type of language is most common. However, just as it is not our task to formulate a new, more concise meaning for words, we cannot hope to psychoanalyze the human race—and that is what it might take to permanently remove this blot on our culture.

Realizing this, we can, of course, be most careful in the adjectives and nouns we use. But what happens when the other fellow hasn't "read the book"? The writer, who is Jewish, is again reminded of a personal experience.

A certain sale was proceeding nicely. The product seemed to fit the prospect's needs, and we were at the point of writing up the order. When the customer asked the price, we replied unhesitatingly, because we knew it was most competitive. Yet when our prospective buyer asked: "Is that your lowest price, or can I jew you down?" we "blew" the sale. We just stopped listening. Nothing in the world was going to make us sell that item to such an uncouth, foul-mouthed individual. In the heat of the moment we forgot that our job was to sell, not educate—no matter how badly the prospect seemed to need it.

The same situation is repeated thousands of times daily in sales contacts. Sometimes, it is not an emotionally laden word, but the manner of speech of the prospect that clogs our "inner ear" and interferes with the listening process. Some accents are a pleasure to hear; others are grating. Some prospects have a real speech impediment for which we may have little tolerance, and others may be less educated, but none of these are any indication that the potential customer is any less willing or able to buy. If you catch yourself listening to *how* the other fellow is talking, you'd best shift channels, because you may miss the all-important signal that he's ready to buy, concerning which we shall have much more to discuss later in this book.

One of the better listening habits you might profitably develop is anticipating what the speaker is going to say. There is some danger here, however, because a little anticipation can be good while too much can be disastrous. Try to remain just a little ahead of the other fellow, though. If he is reciting numbers, "one," "two," "three," "four," for example, anticipate the fact that he will next say "five." If he does, indeed, say "five," you will never forget it, because it proved just how right you were. On the other hand, if he should say "six," you'll never forget that either. You will have listened and learned by the best teaching method known to man—comparison. And comparison works even better when we're just a little wrong.

But watch out! In the southwestern part of the United States, they tell of an Indian legend about a big, bald eagle who lost his mate. After pining away for many months, the eagle flew off into the sky in search of another bird to share his nest. As luck would have it, he found a little lark and brought her home. However, the young lark kept the eagle awake all night saying, "I'm a lark—let's spark. I'm a lark—let's spark."

Well, that was too much for the old bird, so the next day he went in search of a more suitable mate. This time he found a small dove. Once again he was foiled, though, because this second bird wore the old eagle out by saying all night, "I'm a dove—let's make love. I'm a dove—let's make love."

On the third day our determined, if somewhat tired, bird made one last attempt. After searching the skies most of the day, he finally located a suitable-looking *duck*. But, the legend tells us, the eagle's luck was no better. Throughout the night his new mate kept him awake, saying, "I'm a drake—did you make a mistake! I'm a drake—did you make a mistake!"

We can't vouch for the authenticity of the story, of course, but it should cure the reader, once and for all, of any tendency to anticipate too much. To jump from possible fiction to undeniable fact, we can all take lessons from the successful door-to-door salesman. Can any selling job be more difficult? He is meeting the prospect on his or her home grounds, usually without any sign that there is even the vaguest interest in what he's selling. (If you have an office or a store, at least there is the distinct possibility that the person who comes through that door is a potential buyer.) Yet our doorbell pushers, certainly the successful ones, approach each prospect as if she or he *is* going to buy. They do not permit themselves to anticipate failure— that should be too far ahead in anticipation for any sales-man—and so they succeed more often than not.

Total good listening habits are so important for people in all walks of life that one can find examples of "dos" and "don'ts" among professionals in practically any field of endeavor. Politicians in particular seem to have mastered the art quite well. In fact, they have perfected a method of capitalizing on one of the worst listening habits of all—the tendency, common to most of us, to take things too literally.

The next time you ask a friend, "How are you?" stop and really listen for the reply. Better yet, ask him how he feels in front of another friend. Then, when you get the usual "fine" or "okay" for a reply, direct yourself to the third party.

"Did you hear my conversation with our friend?" you might ask.

"Oh, yes," will be the reply.

"Well, what did he say when I asked how he felt?"

"He said that he feels fine."

"Now, honestly, just between us, do you think it possible for anyone to feel truly fine—not to have a single thing bother him."

"Well, no, not exactly. . . ."

"In that case, you'd say that our friend was being polite and diplomatic by telling us that he feels fine. He didn't wish to bother us with some little trouble he has."

"Yes."

"He wasn't being completely truthful."

"You might say that."

At this point, if you want to be a real troublemaker, you can turn to your first friend and ask: "Did you hear him call you a liar?"

This bit of forced play on taking things too literally is a gambit well known to every dictator (political or social)

in the world. It is also a favorite device of some psychiatrists who use it, under controlled circumstances, to get
people angry enough to tell the truth about themselves.
For the salesman who listens for it, the "take it literally"
invitation from a prospect should be a warning.

You may hear it from a potential customer who says,
"Your price is way too high." He's hoping, of course, that
you'll accept that statement at face value without question,
at least in your own mind, as to what "way too high"
means. Once you recognize it, though, it's an easy trap to
avoid.

To a very great degree, all of this is a throwback to the
same problem of people, even when they are not deliberately trying to confuse us, meaning something different
from what we hear. For the salesman earning fifteen thou-
sand dollars or more a year, and depending upon the item
being offered, it might seem that "too high" is another way
of asking for a reduction in price of a couple of hundred
dollars. Yet if the salesman is in the under-eight-thou-
sand-dollar category, even ten dollars could be "too high."
The only possibility of reaching agreement on what was
meant is employing empathy, or "feeling" it the way the
other fellow does, which we mentioned earlier in this
chapter.

Naturally, price is not the only area of potential misunderstanding between salesman and prospect. The problem is so complicated that there is now a large school of
semanticists that believes that there are no "facts." The
only truth, they hold, is based upon experience, and no
two individuals could possibly have experienced all of the
same things. Thus, the color "midnight blue" might well
mean one thing to the salesman and another to the customer. Such expressions as "close tolerance" convey one
thought to the layman, and another to the engineer.

As intriguing as it might be to pursue this subject further, the salesman, fortunately, does not have to make an in-depth study of it. Mere recognition of the differences in the meaning of most words is sufficient for intelligent communication between individuals of good will. When the possibility of misinterpretation does arise, it is relatively easy to fall back upon some mutually acceptable "standard" such as a color chart, ruler, etc. Such things, which can represent a "common language" between individuals, should be in the "tool box" of all communicators.

To be able to fully understand exactly what the other fellow means is a rare but wonderful gift, particularly for the salesman. It is, though, well within the reach of everyone. If you've been listening (reading) so far, you've learned that your own skill can be vastly improved if you will pause occasionally to take stock of the sounds around you. It will help, too, if you make a sincere effort to understand what the originator of those sounds is attempting to communicate. Furthermore, you should be wary of the prejudices of any speaker and of your emotional response to certain words or types of individuals. At the same time, cultivating the abilities to concentrate on what's being said and anticipating—just a little—what the speaker will say next can add to the profitability of any conversation.

If you will, in fact, develop the habit of efficient listening, certain shortcuts to better understanding will present themselves to you. For one thing, it will soon become apparent that practically all speakers attempting to make a point—and this applies to customers or prospects as well as anyone else—tend to do so in three easily definable steps. They will, first of all, state a fact. This will be followed by some sort of generalization. In conclusion, they will tend to get somewhat emotional about the whole thing.

This can be best illustrated with the example of a cus-

tomer who has some complaint—and many a salesman has
been "thrown" off his sales pace by this one. "The whatsit
you sold me last month doesn't work," the customer might
say. However, he'll seldom let it go at that.

To continue with this same example, the prospect for
an add-on or additional sale might add: "We had one of
these many years ago, and, come to think of it, that one
never worked properly either." By now, unless the salesman is really listening, the entire process of communicating
is beginning to fall apart. Attention wanders, fear of a lost
customer sets in, etc. Yet the customer must deliver his
final blow.

"I don't know why I permitted you to talk me into
buying the darn thing in the first place."

What a trap! It is amazing how many otherwise good
listeners will "fall" for conversations of this sort, and waste
their precious energies trying to explain why the unit purchased several months or even years ago might have failed,
or how they really didn't force the customer to buy the
same model again.

In all their excitement, they forget to "hear" the only
significant part of what was said—the present piece isn't
working properly. If they could just mentally zero in on
that one point, they might be able to suggest a simple
solution, such as testing for a blown fuse, an electrical plug
accidentally kicked out of a wall socket, or the correct way
to use the product, which could make the customer happy
again without going through an expensive service call.

To a greater or lesser degree, all of us are guilty of
expanding our remarks into those three divisions—fact,
generalization, and emotional outburst. However, this does
not mean that we have to listen the same way. A good
listener will sort the wheat from the chaff by mentally
making an outline of what the speaker is attempting to say.

He will thereby relegate the generalizations and emotional aspects of the conversation to their proper subordinate roles and concentrate on the point.

Oddly enough, although almost all of us tend to talk too much when we're attempting to put an idea across the communication wall, we'll select words that have the effect of short-circuiting conversation. Most likely this is due in part to our high-speed educational system, which tends to limit our vocabulary. Whatever its background, this tendency is called "abstracting" by semanticists, and they tell us that it's not all bad. Consider how long our conversations would be if we had to describe all of his physical features each time we used the word "man." Surely, in most cases we can get away with "the house" rather than the specific address of the residence, or "the boss" without identifying him by name or rank in the managerial hierarchy. Is it any wonder, therefore, that we say "the darn thing doesn't work" or "we don't want any" and leave it up to the good listener to inquire about the symptoms for the failure or the reasons for not wanting to buy?

In your sales day, you will have ample opportunity to listen for abstractions and even use them yourself. The very name of your product is an abstract of the total of its components. On the other hand, we must accept the fact that salesmen have no monopoly on speech shortcuts. Prospects can use these deliberately to save time or catch a salesman who isn't listening off guard. (We have already seen what damage a tyrant might do with such a harmless abstraction as "I feel fine.") The dialogue that usually takes place between salesman and prospect most often starts with much of the specifics left unspoken. Soon we shall see how profitable it can be to "get down to cases" as rapidly as possible. Before we can do this, it is necessary to recognize abstracts similar to those mentioned when we hear them.

Chapter 4

What Is a "Sale"?

Strange, isn't it, how the things we do most frequently in our daily lives are the most difficult to explain or define. Pressed for an immediate answer, we'd all have trouble stating which side of our face we shave first each morning, or which shoe is the first to be tied. It is even less likely that, without looking at it now, we can tell the color and pattern of the tie we put on this morning. We perform these tasks so often that they have become habits—very much like going to our place of business each day.

Surely, our work-a-day world is cluttered with enough problems without asking why we earn our bread as we do, or what is the precise definition of the task we perform. Or is it? When you get right down to it, can you think of anything more important than knowing why and what we're doing so that we may, at least, tell ourselves? It is possible that, in the telling, some better way of getting the job done will occur to us. If nothing else, when the task is defined we should end up with a clearer concept of the meaning of this part of life.

Yet how many of us who earn our living at this trade can define a "sale"? For some, the business of making "sales" is merely something into which Fate happened to toss them, or is a refuge from another job at which they have failed. For others, it's a way station on the road to a "better" position, but for most it's "just a living" or "an easy way to be in business for yourself without having the capital responsibilities of management."

That last definition is worthy of closer inspection because, whether they realize it or not, a majority of people who make their living selling feel that way about the job. The American spirit of "independence" runs deep. It is part of the early education of most citizens, and, even in these days of great preoccupation with "security," it is still the number-one goal of most of us. Right or wrong, "independence" in the commercial world is epitomized by the one who runs his own business. Many talents other than salesmanship, though, are necessary to be a successful entrepreneur, and comparatively few people have the capital required for investment. All of this, however, does not make the prize any less appealing.

Thanks to the efforts of such renowned industrial psychologists as Professor Abraham H. Maslow of Brandeis University, we now know much more about the "man does not live by bread alone" concept of living. "Only recently has it dawned upon me that as important as education, perhaps even more important, is the work life of an individual, since everybody works," * Professor Maslow journalizes. From this beginning, the professor has formulated a "theory of motivation," which starts with the necessity to satisfy the physical requirements of living and ends with the need to have a personal sense of worth—each forming part of the ladder leading to a task well done. Sensual pleasure gratification and what others think of us are additional steps.

* *Eupsychian Management,* Abraham H. Maslow, Richard D. Irwin, Inc., 1965.

It is true, of course, that there is a certain romance of independence surrounding a sale. For "outside" salesmen, this freedom from close supervision is obvious; but even on a retail sales floor there is no one and nothing between the salesman and the prospect except the product. There is much to be said for the satisfaction that comes from converting that prospect into a customer. Indeed, for many individuals, this sense of fulfillment is so vital that it is unwise, even after they have achieved the highest level of sales efficiency, to "promote" them to a managerial post.

No one can or should attempt to tell a salesman just what his life's work means. We are, admittedly, dealing here with a most subjective definition. The salesman who views his task as a challenge, a contest between himself and the prospect, may well require the bit of additional self-esteem that comes from "winning." Another, seeing himself as an important cog in the organizational wheel, will want to establish the best possible rapport with his prospects—even if that means losing an occasional sale— for "the good of the company." Recognizing that he is the last link between factory and consumer of that particular product, he will see "selling" as a two-way communications network between producer and user, with much to be learned from the reasons why people *don't* buy.

All of these motivating factors, collectively or individually, can operate as well upon the sales prospect. He, too, has certain physical and emotional requirements that will color his view of a sales situation. To a degree greater than that for a salesman, who is trained to forget about yesterday's failures or even the fact that last month he was top man in the organization (there is always a new quota to be met), the prospect will be guided by experience in defining a "sale."

If he has been "burned" in previous sales encounters

with either shoddy merchandise or service, or if he has subsequently discovered that he has paid more than he should have for the purchase, the customer will think of a sale as a disagreeable penalty that we all must pay for living in these days of specialization, when one cannot produce everything he consumes. In short, he will embark upon each "buying" venture with his guard up. On the theory that the best defense is an offense, he may even be antagonistic to the salesman. Without the benefit of having read the last chapter, the prospect is likely to confuse the symbol with the thing being defined, and lump you and every other salesman he meets into the one category of a threat to his pocketbook.

Is it any wonder that these customers feel as they do? Exposure to incompetent salesmen aside for the moment, they are the ones who "must" have a new automobile every few years, even though the old car is functioning smoothly. Yet they resent any reference to industry profiting from "planned obsolescence." Popular literature abounds with articles and books attacking businessmen for deliberately creating "inferior" products in order to keep demand up to the high level of supply, but the technological and functional design achievements are hardly ever mentioned, except in sales promotion literature, because no one will buy a book that tells him he is doing the right thing. Such a situation leaves it squarely up to the salesman to change this consumer concept of a sale.

Fortunately, not all prospects are so soured on sales transactions. Most women consumers, for example, actually enjoy the buying experience, because, being the prime spenders of disposable income in this country, they view each purchase as further justification of their important role in society. As any salesman who caters to this market can testify, this does not make it easy to sell to women.

However, the challenge here is different. The job is to make it easier for these shoppers to do what they want to do.

To this type of prospect, and the group includes both men and women, *you* are the sale. In other words, unless your product is so much in demand or is priced so low as to attract "impulse" purchasing, the customer would find it difficult to define the sale without including you—your appearance, mannerisms, and speech—in the definition.

Once again, the subjective nature of a "sale" becomes apparent, and the fact that each of us thinks of the word in the light of his experiential background is brought home. For an exact definition of "sale" we could, of course, fall back upon the dictionary, which tells us nothing more than that it means "the exchange or transfer of property for money or its equivalent," but this hardly gives us the needed insight for self-improvement. Among other things, it is far from technically correct. Not only property, but services and ideas can be part of a sales transaction. And, as indicated above, before we can conclude or even begin "selling," the prospective buyer must be "sold" on us. It seems that here, too, we have returned to the personal nature of a sale, accenting the magnitude of the task of finding a common, true meaning for the word.

The answer to the all-important question of what "sale" really means to your customers can only be found in the study of semantics, which, as we learned earlier, reminds us to distinguish between the word as a symbol and what is actually being described. By common agreement, we may agree upon a precise definition, but no amount of empathy can ever enable us to see the events symbolized exactly the same way the next person does. The best we can do is try!

In attempting to "see" a sale as your prospect does, you

should bear in mind the principle of "abstraction" also mentioned in Chapter 3. Remember that this is a most personal matter. While our grade-school study of a language teaches us the dictionary meaning of the word—i.e., a sale, basically, is the exchange of property for money— later events in our lives shape and reshape our concepts so that the final abstraction is quite different for each of us. To better understand how this works, you would do well to consider the process very much like a step ladder with the formal definition on the lowermost rung.

Step two, depending upon individual experience, could very well be recollection of the last purchase, or the largest purchase your customer made. He could have spent this money with you or with some other salesman. It may even conjure up subconscious thoughts of something this person wants but cannot afford to buy. The vital point is that, to him, the word "sale" is related to a specific item and/or transaction either in the past or projected future.

According to Maslow, this step is not too easy for the average salesman to understand. The professor's studies of men who earn their living selling lead him to state that these businessmen work within a shorter time span than others. He notes that salesmen, characteristically, keep their eyes focused on the next deal. For them, living in the present means the next few hours or days at the most. However, Maslow envisions the day when all those who sell, even though they be employees, think of their company as if they owned it and were preparing to pass it along to their heirs.

Step three. Money, to pick up another part of our dictionary definition of a "sale," certainly is quickly abstracted by most people unless they are so insecure that they hoard it for its own sake. To the youngster on an allowance, a dollar could represent a ticket to a movie with something left over for candy. Later, it may mean a vacation or some other reward for doing a good job. Even when it is retained in the bank, money or the numbers in the passbook stand for security. In any case, it seldom if ever is used to paper the walls.

It is not too difficult to visualize a moneyless society. Many people around the world, including over half a million in the United States, still follow the practice of bartering their goods or services for the goods or services of another. (The hungry tramp who offers to trade an hour or two of lawn-mowing or wood-chopping for a meal is an example that comes to mind.) Furthermore, this exchange, among certain ethnic groups, is marked by a great deal of religiosity, and the individual who gives something more valuable than that which he receives is held in high esteem. The potlatch ceremony of our northwestern coast Indians is a case in point, but you don't have to look farther than the neighbors who come to dinner bearing a gift worth far more than the food for an example closer to home. The whole point is that, even in our society, money, unless it will buy something, is worthless, and its value, obviously, increases in proportion to the value of what it will buy.

Step four. Continuing up the ladder of abstraction from our basic definition of our business task, we come to the word "property." If ever there was a word wide open to numerous subjective interpretations, this is it. To a native of any one of hundreds of African tribes, a wife is considered "property" in very much the same vein as we think of our automobiles. And, as every schoolboy knows, Shakespeare looked upon money as "trash," but viewed one's "good name" as the most valuable of possessions. Within our contemporary society, we tend to avoid these extremes. "Salesmen" who trade in women are properly imprisoned, and, although one's reputation is still held in high regard

in some places and a multibillion dollar industry—
advertising and public relations—has been built around the
sale of this intangible, it is still small when compared with
the rest of the economy. Yet, none can deny that publicity
and such things as the expertise of a lawyer or accountant
are very real, and worth considerable money in the market
place.

The distinction between different types of "property"
and the variations in the meaning of the word to individual
prospects are the most important bits of knowledge a salesman can possess. Another way of considering these differences is to think of the world in which we live and the
problems—from finding food to searching for happiness—
that confront all of us daily. Surely, only a true glutton
would argue that those two problems are one and the same.

The vast majority would recognize that a solution to the
first, or acquiring sufficient food, has a degree of what has
been called "instrumental" usefulness, because it is a
means to an end—in this instance sustaining life. In this
light, the exact worth of the property that enables us to
solve that problem is directly proportional to the value we
place on our lives. For most of us, it would probably be
impossible to place a top figure on that value. What can
be more important than life? Yet there is no doubt that
it does have its limits, as witness the number of people
who have willingly died for a cause, sacrificed themselves
for a loved one, etc. We surely must agree that the best
bread salesman in the world would not have increased his
income one bit through trade with Mohandas Gandhi
during one of his politically inspired fasts.

However, we don't have to go to such extremes to find
examples of property that can be considered to be of instrumental value or useful for some purpose other than its own
being, just as the instrumental worth of money lies in the

fact that it enables us to accumulate other things, which, hopefully, lead to happiness. With wealth, we buy automobiles for riding, chairs for sitting, clothes for wearing, etc. Undoubtedly, you can find some instrumental value in whatever it is you're selling.

"Not so fast," you might well argue. "How about some of those very same products that are purchased, not for what someone can do with them, but just because they look nice or make a better impression on the neighbors?" You can and should point to the fact, already noted, that Americans in particular replace many items long before they are too old and worn to perform their utilitarian function.

The point is well taken. But happiness, to take one example, is no less a need of the human animal than is food. In this case, though, the need may be said to be "intrinsic," or an end in itself rather than "instrumental" in moving us toward a desired goal. To love one's job as a salesman so much that the money earned is of secondary importance is another example of this intrinsic value. Believe it or not, many salesmen do feel that way about their work, and almost all prospects have, at least, one "final" goal in mind, such as pleasure or status, that they feel is worth pursuing. Any one of these aims can be part of the "property of the mind" that a potential customer hopes to take home from the sales experience. A good salesman will find out for certain.

Step five. By definition, the word "exchange" means at least two parties to the transaction, and more important, it implies a certain freedom of choice. Let us never forget that! In this "free" economy, you and your customer do have an option. Unless there is some evidence of discrimination against an individual prospective buyer, there is no law that compels a salesman to sell to anyone. (We are not concerned here with the voluminous federal legislation governing such things as discriminatory price concessions in selling, except to note its existence and advise all those engaged in such transactions to be familiar with these laws.) Likewise, there is no statute requiring a prospect to buy from a specific firm or salesman. For all intents and purposes, therefore, the two are free to deal with each other at arm's length.

As we shall discover in the next chapter, buyers base their decisions more on emotional than rational factors, just as salesmen feel more comfortable in the presence of one customer rather than another and will tend to make more "calls" on the prospect with whom they have this warmer relationship. In each instance, the "exchange" arouses some emotion, whether we realize it or not. A child who has been bullied or ignored by a shopkeeper may, thereafter, dread going to the store for his parent, even as any adult customer who has been abused or taken advantage of by a salesman will tend to shy away from again placing himself in such a situation.

It is not your task, of course, to police the entire profession of selling. At the same time, you cannot afford to ignore the fact that people deal with many salesmen in their lives. Their attitude towards the thought of this "exchange" will be colored by the people they've met. If the experience has been bad or distasteful, the very word "salesman" can be a negative factor you will have to overcome.

For this reason, among others, the professional eliminates such phrases as "What can I sell you?" or "I'm here to sell you . . ." from his business vocabulary. If we accept the premise that an individual acts more out of emotion than reason, it follows, logically, that we cannot reason someone out of a conclusion arrived at based on emotion.

What is the sense of sending a "salesman" to "sell" even the most valuable of products to a prospect who may not be able to stand the sound of either word? No, we must use whatever little knowledge we have about emotional impact to appeal to a prospect on a more pleasant level, even if it involves a simple greeting such as "How may I serve you?" to take this particular experience out of the category of all other sales situations in which the prospect may have found himself.

By now the reader can surely appreciate the fact that arriving at a working definition of "sale" is no easy matter. It is, nevertheless, more than just an academic exercise. Before we can set out on any journey, we must know our destination or goal. It should be crystal clear not only as to name, but as to what we shall experience and see when we get there. In this way, and only in this way, will we be able to make the necessary changes in our speed and direction of travel to overcome the roadblocks inevitably placed in our path. As we stated in Chapter 1, it is not too soon to keep our eyes upon the fence rather than just upon the hole.

The chief difficulty is that people simply do not use standard dictionary definitions for words they employ to describe activities of the sort we have been considering. Many shoppers who admittedly enjoy buying nevertheless refer to their encounters with a salesman as a "pain in the neck." This is not so hard to understand when we recall that an entire branch of medicine (psychosomatics) is based on the assumption that the emotional stresses of everyday living may be felt as physical pain. Some salesman, practicing his art without much thought, may truly succeed in giving his customer a pain in the neck or in some other part of his anatomy. Naturally, it's not you, but watch out for the other fellow and the mess he's made of your prospect.

At the same time, it is relatively easy to recall the pleasure we all got out of going on shopping tours when we were younger and less sophisticated, which is another way of saying less buffeted or hardened by the stupid, cruel, and inhuman actions of which others are capable. None of us are so old that we can't recall the pleasant smell of something new . . . the shining finish . . . the crisp, crinkly feeling of a freshly unwrapped fabric . . . the way our worries and cares were submerged in the romance of the story the salesman wove around the product . . . the pride we felt when we paraded our purchase before our contemporaries . . . or the sense of satisfaction we felt when we realized that, because we had labored so long and so hard, this prize was ours. In other words, in those days a "sale" or buying experience was really "fun." There is no reason why it cannot be that again, provided salesmen will accept the responsibility for making it so.

Abstracting a sale, as we have just done, is one way to discover the prospect's "funnybone," or the point at which he will start enjoying the business at hand. Another way of accomplishing this vital task is to visualize the sales transaction as a gigantic scale, an arm pivoted at the center with two baskets, one at each end. If we can picture the salesman at one basket and the prospective buyer at the other, each piling the good he expects to get out of the deal into his container, we get an entirely new concept of a sale.

By this definition, *a sale is an exchange of goods or benefits.* If the scale is weighted in favor of either the salesman or customer, the transaction cannot be concluded without one or the other deriving a greater amount of benefit. This is not the type of sale we're after! On the other hand, when the scales are perfectly in balance—when the weight that both parties attach to the deal is equal—a sale will take place.

If we are to truly understand this definition, we must first advance our thinking in a different direction, and turn our thoughts to yet another question. We should ask ourselves: "What is good?"

This query, as it applies to motives and benefits in business, is not new. Men have been addressing themselves to it since at least the Middle Ages, when the Church was the prime source of answers to such philosophical questions. Turning their attention to the then-emerging form of capitalistic economy, the leaders of that time decreed, for example, that not only usury but avarice in the form of buying for less than the next fellow paid was sinful or bad. In fact, the very practices of manufacturing or wholesaling, as witness the writings of the master theologian of the day, St. Thomas Aquinas, were highly suspect, with the latter type of enterprise the most sinful of all. "Whosoever buys a thing, not that he may sell it whole and unchanged, but that it may be a material for fashioning something, he is no merchant," St. Thomas wrote. "But the man who buys it in order that he may gain by selling it again unchanged and as he bought it, that man is of the buyers and sellers who are cast forth from God's temple."

Today, of course, there is no such stigma attached to wholesaling, but the question of what is right and good remains. Hayakawa, mentioned earlier, notes that our thinking on this subject sometimes takes the form of "two-valued" orientation, or the tendency, which we all have to a degree, to classify things or ideas as either "right" or "wrong," or "good" or bad." He traces this very human trait to the earliest history of man, when survival depended to a large extent on adopting this "all or nothing" attitude. There was no time to weigh the *degree* of danger that was always present, and so impulsive thought or action with a corresponding increase in heartbeat and adrenal flow—the better to run or stand and fight—became a normal, necessary way of life.

Modern man, somewhat restricted in the socially acceptable forms of striking back at a supposed "enemy" or even expressing "love," has chosen a different set of weapons or tools—words. However, the habit of thinking in terms of absolutes remains. It is still safer and certainly easier to classify people and things as "good" or "bad" rather than "fairly good" or "not so bad." The latter form of expression requires a degree of understanding and comparative judgment that, even if we elect to devote the necessary time to making them, leaves us more vulnerable to attack from two extremes. At least, if we say that something is "good," only those who think that it is "bad" can disagree. But, as every peacemaker knows, to say just "pretty good" may bring criticism from both those who think it's good and those who think it's bad.

A case in point would be demonstrations against a government. The typical citizen responds to these either favorably or unfavorably. It all seems to depend upon the attitude of his peer group. Few have the courage to express thoughts contrary to the belief of friends, and fewer still will risk incurring the animosity of business associates. Even among those who say, "Yes, but . . ." there is every reason to believe that the object is not so much to be fair, but to hedge their remarks so that whichever way the situation evolves they will come out on the winning side.

Somewhat less controversial but every bit as important to our study here is the example of the customer who is asked to comment on the taste of a particular brand of cigarette. He will either like it or he won't. Here we will encounter very few half-hearted statements. This is due to a number of factors. First, there are so many other brands from which he can choose that he can afford to be intolerant of one. Second, he doesn't wish to give the impression that he can't make up his mind, so he'll risk a declaration one way or another. After all, you'll either agree with him or you won't.

In contrast to all of this is that segment of our society which can be said to be oriented along "multivalued" lines. Another way of putting this would be to say that these are individuals who have the enviable capacity to judge not in terms of absolutes but in degrees. For them, water is hardly ever "hot" or "cold" but may be "extremely hot" or "cool," and they possess a perfect understanding of the comparative meaning of such adjectives as "extremely," "very," "quite," etc. They realize better than most that there are few "goods" in this world, with the possible exception of those things which have an intrinsic value to them. Therefore, the weight they assign to factors influencing a sale is comparative with all of the subjective reference taken into consideration.

With this background, the reader can easily imagine how difficult it is to list what is "good" in any sales transaction. However, the effort is worthwhile, because, as we have stated, the journey (to success) is much easier when we have the goal clearly in mind. Naturally, it is highly unlikely that any two individuals will see exactly the same "good" in a deal, nor will the same "good" always appeal to one person. Let's begin, though, by thinking of the salesman's side of the scale, and the benefits he hopes to derive from the transaction.

Money, despite or because of our earlier references to it as being of "instrumental" value, is surely one of the things the seller hopes to take home from the party. The reader is again reminded, however, that the precise amount involved depends, for the most part, on what the seller expects to do with the money. If, for instance, the salesman expects to use his commission on this particular sale to purchase a new automobile, it would make just as much sense to reduce the cost of the item to a buyer who offers to barter an acceptable car. Obviously, most of the time transactions of this sort are impractical, so an amount of currency is agreed upon, and it is expected that these dollars will enable both the salesman and his firm to realize a genuine "good" from the sale.

For some reason, the company's position in the transaction we've been considering is often overlooked by both the salesman and prospect. It hovers in the background, neatly framing the sales picture, but it is hardly ever given the consideration it deserves. One possible explanation is that, unless the salesman is also the owner, the "business" is a distant, impersonal thing. Certainly the salesman recognizes it as the fountainhead of his security; however, a much-too-large number share with their customers the misbelief that all businesses have more money than they know what to do with. At least they feel that any loss in revenue at the sale will be made up in some mysterious "elsewhere." Let's lay that bit of fiction to rest once and for all.

It would be well for a salesman, no less than for any other member of the organization, to be familiar with the firm's operating statement, which indicates whether the business is being run at a profit or a loss. In lay terms, this is simply a listing of all the money taken in and spent. One doesn't have to be an accountant to appreciate the fact that the selling price of an item (plus all other items sold) less all expenses, including the cost of material purchased for resale and selling expenses among others, should result in a profit. And this profit, which commences with the sale, is a return on the owner's investment, a concept that keeps any business in a capitalistic economy running.

Contrary to what many salesmen think, meeting competition is not the way the truly worthwhile lines are priced. In fact, this is the surest path to bankruptcy. Better-run businesses determine their selling prices and sales quotas by budgeting for a return on investment, or determining what the owners can reasonably expect to earn on the money or capital they spend for such things as material and salaries or commissions. If, for example, savings banks or other such comparatively safe places to invest money are paying the investor 5 to 6 percent, the businessman, taking greater risks, has a right to anticipate a greater return.

Then, even before the first sale is made, the business capital available is multiplied by the percentage return desired. This establishes the dollar profit that the enterprise expects to make. Looking at the market and costs of doing business realistically, the owners will next divide the dollars they hope to earn by the percentage net profit on sales they hope to realize. Depending upon the type of business, this can be anywhere from 3 to 10 percent before taxes. In any case, the final figure is a sales goal for the firm and, of course, provides the basis for establishing quotas for individual salesmen.

This business of pricing for a profit could lead us into an entirely new, fascinating area of study. It would surely not be a waste of time for the salesman reader to pursue it further, because the knowledge of how prices are determined leads to greater confidence on the sales floor when the subject comes up—as it invariably does. However, in the interest of pressing ahead with our analysis of other aspects of a sale, we shall drop the topic here with the final caution that prices, in organizations with a future, are not the whim of any individual or group. They are calculated to insure the fact that the business will be around to serve and service its customers for a long time to come.

Anyone who has ever earned his living selling will recognize that another "good" on the seller's side of the scale is the personal satisfaction that comes from a job well done. We are not considering, here, the impact of success on one's standing in the community. That will come later. Rather, we're zeroing in on the sheer joy of "winning," which we develop very early in life—perhaps as early as when we first reached out and discovered that something was within reach of our infant grasp.

This "drive" for success seems never to desert us. In adult life, the sources of satisfaction take different forms, but the object—approval of oneself—remains the same. Indeed, it has been philosophically argued that, in a very real sense, all of life is a contest and all of us enjoy being winners. Sooner or later, naturally, we must lose that final battle. Yet, the very knowledge that we are mortal, an insight that seems to be peculiar to mankind, makes us all the more determined to win while we're alive. It's a perfectly normal desire, provided we keep "winning" in its proper perspective.

Of late, this subject has been receiving considerable attention from psychiatrists and psychoanalysts who recognize that an overdeveloped "drive" can be a neurotic symptom of some more serious disorder. We are all acquainted with individuals who, despite the physically comfortable lives they lead, "push" themselves and their families to the point where they no longer relate to society. It does little good to ask these people how many steaks they can eat, because, either out of force of habit or to fill some fancied emotional void in their lives, they keep up the pressure on themselves.

In more "normal" individuals, the doctors have concluded, contests "won" are mentally and emotionally stored for countering the periods of depression that tend to overcome even the best-adjusted of us when we "lose." The salesman who has successfully closed a particularly difficult sale can draw upon that experience when he loses another one, or even when he encounters an impossible social situation. "I can't be all bad," our hero can truthfully tell himself. "I did make that tough sale."

The reader will undoubtedly recognize this as the principal ingredient of the self-confidence without which no salesman can face a prospect. It is a way of life that can be beneficial to everyone, and even to those highly impersonal companies. As a matter of fact, one of the best social messages of our time is the "if you got it, flaunt it" theme of a national advertiser. The advice is equally applicable to individuals who tend to go through life dwelling upon their failures rather than upon their successes. Either way, the opinion of self has a way of coming through. It is reflected in the way one talks, walks, or just how attentive he is to the task at hand. If the failures dominate one's personality, other people tend to avoid him, because they are afraid that some of it will rub off on them. Success, though, breeds success. Everyone wants to be identified with a winner.

The plain fact is that it's easier to rationalize buying from a "winning" salesman because everyone else is doing it. And that is a "good" that every salesman can get from the last sale he closed.

"Winners," of course, get another reward—the approbation of their contemporaries. Although some people pretend to make light of it, seeing their name at the head of a sales contest chart is most gratifying. Among other things, it serves to establish one in the eyes of friends and family as a person who is making a major contribution to the community. But winning out over competition has more tangible rewards, and here, once again, the difference between man and other creatures in the primate category is accented.

Zoologists, who make a study of such things, tell us that there are just two reasons why animals compete with other members of their own species. First, there is a desire to establish dominance over some piece of territory, whether it be a watering hole or a tree. And second, there is the attempt to achieve a higher position in the social order of the tribe or society with all of the advantages, like taxing other members or mating with the choicest females, that accrue to the "top dog." It is not too difficult to realize that, although he has more sophisticated ways of expressing these ambitions, man also fights for these same goals with everything from wars to sales contests, but then he adds a third dimension that is somewhat uniquely his own.

Within the geography staked out by his group, man has a subterritory for which he will do battle. This extra domain is known as a "household." It results from the evolution of man to our present concept of him as a cooperative hunter operating out of a home base. Protecting and even expanding that base—going from a two-room flat to a multiroom house in the country, if you will—are additional reasons for waging the good fight. Sometimes, as when the household is threatened by an intruder, man will fight with every animal instinct remaining. (The thin veneer of civilization quickly falls away when there is a burglar on the premises.) More often, though, the battle is fought on the business field with a completed sale, representing such things as job security or extra compensation, the trophy to be brought home.

Money, self-esteem, and all the tangible and intangible rewards of beating our competition are not the only "goods" a salesman gains from a sale. The reader, considering his own motives, can probably think of others. For instance, some sellers who have considered the instrumental and intrinsic value of their products realize a certain satisfaction from bringing these to a buyer. All of us cannot experience the sense of fulfillment that a doctor feels when he saves a life, or that an attorney realizes when he is instrumental in upholding justice. However, appreciation of the happiness a customer can add to his life by purchasing your wares can be just as rewarding if you think of how dull existence would be without them.

All of these "goods," individually or in combination with each other, go into the balance. To keep the scale level, the prospective customer must take away as many, but no more, benefits. Now, let's analyze some of those consumer "goods" in greater detail than many of us have ever done before.

Chapter 5

Why People Buy— or Don't Buy

Can you recall the days when selling was a simple affair?

If you had something another person might want, your first order of business was to make him know that you had it, and the second was to agree upon a price. Those were the days before "motivation" became a part of everybody's vocabulary and when the business of psychology remained in the hands of professionals, who were concerned with more important matters than which shade of toilet tissue had the greatest impact on the supermarket shopper. Of course, that was also the time when, despite a population that was one-third smaller than today's, there just weren't enough jobs available for all those willing to work. Because of that, individuals lucky enough to find work labored sixty to seventy-two hours a week for the bare necessities of life. Most of our present-day, comfort-giving products were not available at any price. Even the most cynical of us will have to admit that mankind, at least in this country, has progressed to a far better physical environment.

The lessons of this progress are important not only to sociologists, but to salesmen as well. Unless we subscribe to the theory, popular in some quarters, that the evolution of our society has ceased, and that we are entrapped by a way of life predicated upon wars that must, one day, destroy us all, we should look ahead to still shorter work weeks and more conveniences. The key to selling in those still happier days can be found in a study of the current market, which finds most factory workers living in more luxurious surroundings than did the moneyed aristocracy of a century ago.

Closer examination reveals that the chief reason for all of this affluence lies in the technological, mass-producing efficiency of American industry. Whereas the cost of producing a pair of shoes, for example, only a short while ago represented a week's wages for the average workingman, today, even with inflationary pressures on the economy, the cost is less than an hour's time. We have, in effect, learned how to get more out of our human resources, and this rate of increased efficiency is now running at slightly over 3 percent each year. Barring any major upheaval, the next generation will produce twice the number of items currently being manufactured with no more human energy than we are now expending.

This better way of life, and we must surely call it that, is not without its cost. And perhaps the highest price we are paying is the tremendous pressures on all sales forces to dispose of the endless stream of products coming off our assembly lines. We simply can't have mass production without mass consumption. It is a never-ending cycle of lower prices bringing more people into the market place, and the increased demand leading to greater production, bringing still lower prices, etc., etc.

Unsure of their market and working with untried production methods, the first producers of pocket transistor radios, for instance, were compelled to offer them to the public for upwards of fifty dollars. Now, a scant decade later, with perfected mass production techniques and a market broad enough to accept almost everything that's manufactured, the unit price of this item is one-tenth of what it was.

Another case in point is the home refrigerator industry, which, despite rising costs of labor and raw material, has succeeded in reducing prices to 90 percent of what they were in 1957. The genius of these manufacturers, which has enabled us to place a refrigerator in virtually every household in the United States, is reflected in an annual production rate of some 5 million units. Producing less, with the large fixed investment in factory equipment, would surely raise the unit price to the consumer. This would be most unwise for an entire industry, and ruinous for one firm, which would, thereby, price itself out of the market. We are, in effect, prisoners of a system of pricing based upon selling everything that can be most economically produced, rather than manufacturing only the number of items that can be sold.

This is not to say that salesmen should have no voice in production plans. Indeed, the opposite is intended. It would be foolhardy these days for the engineers to apply themselves to perfecting some inexpensive method for turning out large quantities of something like buggy whips. With its supposed better knowledge of the market, the sales staff would be in the best position to advise against that. But once the die is cast, selling becomes an important extension of the distribution arm, which leads from factory to consumer with price smoothing the way. That this represents a joint effort by all should be apparent.

For all these reasons, the entire business organization

is concerned with the subject of why people buy, or don't buy. The answers here have a direct and profound bearing upon the entire economy. However, due to his position in the forefront of the merchandising line, the salesman should be the first to get the message. This, at the same time, can be a most fascinating and frightening experience.

Obviously, the realization that we might learn something that will better enable us to trigger the "buy" mechanism during the sale is most intriguing, especially if our livelihood is at stake. Yet, if we are to be perfectly honest in our search for knowledge, we must begin by accepting the fact that, with few if any exceptions, our customers could survive without our products or services. That could be a most traumatic lesson for a less-than-mature salesman.

The time to start facing up to this truth has long since passed. Salesmen in a democratic society, no matter how affluent the group as a whole might be, can never escape the burden of choice enjoyed by the customer. Not only can he choose between one brand of a product and another, he may elect not to buy it at all. We have already seen how even the food salesman must contend with the possibility that individuals, for reasons ranging from political to religious, may simply decide not to eat. The fact that comparatively few people are driven to this extreme does not make the problem any less significant. In our country, which produces enough foodstuffs to feed more than three times the population, the task of the salesman is to get people to eat more than they absolutely need. (Presently we shall see that this is neither unethical nor intellectually dishonest.) In this, of course, we have succeeded very nicely, as witness the 40 percent of the nation that is overweight or obese.

Critics who may cite this very example of the evils of

"overselling" are either naive or shortsighted. They ignore the fact that each of us is free to eat or not eat as his stomach and conscience dictate. Furthermore, they forget about the multimillion dollar reducing-pill and physical-exercise industries that evolved out of this very problem. If we ever stop to moralize over the sale of any product, except those which in any quantity are physically or emotionally injurious, we shall be compelled to return to living off forest vegetation with none of the conveniences of contemporary life.

Why, then, do people buy more than they need to keep skin and bones together? The answer, as we indicated in the last chapter, is that they expect to get a "good" out of the transaction. Before we begin to examine these "goods" in detail, it is necessary to recall that in dealing with the human being we are relating to a most complicated creature, and that our task is not made easier by the fact that we are, ourselves, human. In both cases, there are two distinct forces that are brought to bear upon the relationship.

The first of these is the cool, calculating mind of the individual, which could tell him to shop for a new car. "Your old one is unsafe," it might say. "True, you could put it in a state of good repair, but there is every chance that, because of its overall age and mileage run, another part will soon fail. You have, therefore, two logical choices: either buy a new car or start walking."

Residing within this same individual is an equally potent emotional force that may act either independently or in conjunction with the logical one. "I'll be damned if I'll buy a new car now," it could say. "The children use it most of the time, and they have no appreciation of how hard I have to work to support these luxuries. If they want a

car, let them buy it. I can always walk, and besides, the
exercise might do me good."

Here we have an insight into a fairly typical buying
decision. To buy or not to buy, that is the question. It
should be noted that the direction finally taken is influenced by both the need affirmed ("Your old car is unsafe")
and the need disowned ("I can always walk"). The wise
salesman will recognize that this inner struggle is taking
place in every prospect he encounters, and he will remain
on the alert for ways to bolster the need affirmed. At the
same time he will appreciate the fact that sheer logic is
not always on his side.

In the example just cited, the emotional mind might
have said yes even while the rational section of the brain
was dictating no. Our automobile prospect, even after
acknowledging that the cost of putting the old jalopy in
shape would be less than the cost of a new car, could
decide to go into the market anyway. "Because the kids
really deserve it. And, after all, the real reason why I'm
working so hard is to better afford the finer things in life."
You see, it always depends upon the point of view, and
no one can state for certain which viewpoint will prevail.
The best we can do is start hammering away at the different buying motives, both rational and emotional, and wait
for some signal from the prospect that we have struck a
responsive chord. Fortunately, the list of possible reasons
why anyone buys anything is not so long that it cannot
be used in its entirety if necessary in any sale.

We have already touched upon one of these customer
"goods"—*status.*

If standing in the community, among his family and
friends and in his own eyes, is important to the salesman,
it is no less so to his prospect. Just how much the customer
is willing to pay in the form of the "goods" he throws into

the sales scale for this prestige will, naturally, vary from sale to sale. There is no doubt, however, that it ranks high on the list of why transactions are successfully completed. Indeed, it has been estimated that over 10 percent of the buying public can be classified as "status buyers," or individuals who purchase things *primarily* on the basis of how their new possession will appear to others.

Although it is not our intention here to moralize, the author cannot suppress the observation that many authorities deplore this state of affairs in the market place. The celebrated psychoanalyst and author Eric Fromm, for one, terms ours a "marketing-oriented" society, or one in which a person's worth is measured less by his thoughts and intrinsic good deeds than by his contribution to the economy. He deplores the pressures on modern man of advertising and "high pressure" salesmanship to buy this or that product "because everyone is doing it," or "because none but a select few can afford it."

According to Fromm, some people succumb to this propaganda in the vain hope that it will win them the love and respect that is otherwise denied to them. Others, and this is the real danger in sales campaigns built strictly around a status-seeking appeal, may discover that the contemplated purchase produces a conflict between what the salesman is saying or implying and what they know to be true—the approval of people who measure others solely by their physical possessions just isn't worth winning. In this case, unless the salesman quickly re-establishes his integrity in some other manner, the sale will be lost. And in the first instance, after the sale is made and the customer finds that it does not bring the hoped-for results, the salesman and his product will bear the brunt of the buyer's disappointment.

Such criticisms of the status-buying motive may well be

valid, but they tell us little more than that people should not behave as they do. On the other hand, the business world is full of examples of how important recognition of this human frailty can be to a successful organization. To mention just one: the largest retailing firm in the country, Sears Roebuck, has captured over one-third of the national market for home clothes washers and dryers, but less than one-tenth of the home entertainment business. The apparent lesson here is that the public is less concerned about the brand name on a product used in the basement or laundry room than it is of the impression made by items in the living room. It is equally clear that this message has not been lost on the management of the chain, and that they are wasting little time in attempting to amend the situation. Currently the company has embarked upon a national advertising campaign picturing prominent personalities with Sears products in their living rooms.

Closely related to the status motive for buying, yet distinctly apart from it, is the *hedonistic* "good" that more and more Americans are deriving from their purchases. The word "hedonism" is representative of the thinking of certain ancient Greek philosophers who held that pleasure, of whatever kind, is the only good. For centuries, while individuals toiled to provide the necessities of life for themselves and for their families, and to save for their old age, this philosophy remained in limbo. Now, spurred by a society that is offering to almost all of its citizens cradle-to-the-grave security, it has again become popular. There are some who believe that the swing has been prompted, too, by the uncertainties of the Atomic Age, in which all of us live under the constant threat of annihilation. Is it any wonder, these analysts inquire, that an increasingly large number of our people have adopted the "I might as well get it while I can" attitude?

Whatever the reason, hedonism is once more a way of life for a substantial portion of the population. It is manifested in the record amount of private debt that has accompanied the expansion of the economy, and the number of items purchased by consumers on impulse. Nowhere is this better illustrated than in the typically American "supermarket" approach to merchandising. Originally, these markets attracted price-conscious shoppers because it was correctly believed that the benefits of mass buying could be passed along to the consumer. Unable to refute this argument, the independent corner grocer all but disappeared from the American landscape. Now a curious change has taken place on supermarket shelves. Instead of only lower-priced staple merchandise, they also offer an array of expensive, exotic foods all handsomely packaged to catch the shopper's eye. That they have succeeded is evidenced by the fact that gross profits in these establishments have climbed almost 8 percent in the past ten years.

Unfortunately, all of us cannot tie our products in a pretty bow and place them on a shelf to sell themselves. Still, we can take advantage of the hedonistic approach in another manner, if we remember that this is just one of several possible buying motives.

Credit has become such a big business in this country, with its ready availability leading to more impulse buying, that Congress has recently felt compelled to establish rules or guidelines for its use. "Buying on time" is now the "in" thing, and the successful salesman is prepared to make it easier for his customers to do just that. If he is calling on a prospect, he has obtained his credit manager's approval beforehand, so that the subject of payment need never come up. If he is operating a retail store, he makes the granting of credit so emotionally painless that the prospect hardly knows that her application is being taken. Remember! It all boils down to making it easier for your customer to do what he or she enjoys doing anyway.

The fact that status and hedonism are difficult "goods" to measure makes them no less real. Also, as we have pointed out, it is not the salesman's job to evaluate such motives. It should suffice to accept their existence and place them somewhere in the balance of a sale.

Most salesmen, though, will probably find it more to their taste to consider reasons for buying that they freely admit using themselves when they are in the position of a customer. To illustrate this point, it would be a good exercise to ask yourself why you made *your* last purchase. The chances are excellent that high on the list of answers from all our readers would be *comfort* or *convenience*. Naturally, you wish a better life for yourself, even as your customer does.

Once more, though, we must bear in mind that not all products lend themselves to an appeal based on all "goods." It is difficult to imagine, for example, a steam-shovel buyer being motivated by a sales talk based on the comfort-giving advantages of the item. On the other hand, in our list of *all* the basic reasons why people buy things, we cannot ignore comfort or convenience. There are simply too many products whose only reason for existence is that they make life easier. In addition, it is entirely feasible that something you consider to be a status symbol or an item to be bought on impulse may be viewed as a comfort-giving necessity by your prospect.

The price we pay for things and services that, strictly speaking, are not essential to the preservation of life, but that are, nevertheless, nice to have around, reflects the high cost of "civilization." Undoubtedly, our species could survive without the automobile, automatic washer, range, vacuum cleaner, and all the other devices—both within and outside the household—that are the hallmark of our time. As a matter of fact, there is some foundation to the suspicion that mankind is not yet emotionally equipped to properly utilize the extra time these products afford him. The picture of the harried businessman rushing to earn money, to buy more time-saving devices, so that he can have more time to earn more money, is all too vivid. Even if we agree with this concept of twentieth-century man, we can hardly expect the salesman alone to provide a solution to this most unhappy situation.

Man's search for ways and means to make life a bit more bearable is certainly not new. The celebrated zoologist Desmond Morris, author of *The Naked Ape,** points out that man, like all mammals and birds, has himself evolved a high, constant body temperature calculated to enable him to function at maximum physiological efficiency. This temperature, in a healthy person, varies no more than a few degrees regardless of the outside temperature. A wider swing is correctly interpreted as an indication of failing health. Furthermore, our bodies also contain built-in mechanisms to maintain this delicate balance. Approximately two million sweat glands help to keep our bodies from overheating, and a similar system of constricting the blood-carrying organs within us enables us to preserve body heat during exposure to cold. The discomfort we experience when these nature's helpers are brought to bear is merely a sign that the proper adjustment is taking place.

As Morris correctly notes, the development of fire, clothing, and insulated homes has also combated heat loss, just as ventilation and refrigeration has been used against heat gain. These inventions in all their forms, of course, do not alter internal body temperature. Yet they do serve to control the environment so that we can continue to

*McGraw-Hill Book Co., 1967.

function at maximum efficiency in a more diverse range of external conditions, with a minimum of discomfort. Comfort and convenience, too, are subjective words. They never always mean the same to any two individuals. Your prospect may, indeed, anticipate his purchase making life "easier," but his understanding of the word is definitely different from yours. Fortunately, now that you have mastered the art of listening, you are in a position to know exactly what the buyer considers comfortable or convenient. The clue may be minimal. It may appear in the passing mention of a hobby or the sweat on his brow, but it is surely there. All you have to do is stop, look, and listen.

When you get right down to it, can you imagine a more universal buyer's "good" than *health?* There's hardly a prospect who cannot be stopped and whose interest will not be aroused by the simple statement: "This will enable you to live longer." As evidenced by the astronomical amount of money Americans spend on medical care, patent medicines, etc., this "good" probably outweighs all others. It can also be seen in the large number of people, of all ages, who read newspaper obituary pages. This preoccupation with life and death is another trait that has been with us for some time. However, more often than not, people will not admit to it. Even the hypochondriac will rationalize his abnormal concern with his health as something other than the fear of death. The average person is not much different, except that he is so well adjusted that frank appeals to his desire to remain healthy are reasonably considered. We must always remember, though, that even the most mature of us consider any abrupt confrontation with the thought of death as being in poor taste.

All of this places a big responsibility on the salesman. The object is to sell the life-preserving benefits of your product without scaring the devil out of the prospect.

Dishwasher sales campaigns saying that their product will enable you to "wash dishes in water hotter than you would put your hands" are a good example of how to walk this thin line. Yet, an automobile advertising program based upon a realistic demonstration of how well the car stood up in a head-on collision was properly abandoned as being "unsaleable."

If you are considering the health appeal as part of your sales message, it is particularly important that you be prepared to follow the lead of your prospect. While this is good advice for all sales situations, and will be more thoroughly explored later, it is emphasized here because it is almost impossible to back away from a mistake in overselling health as a benefit. Once your prospect's senses are offended, your only option is to disown the earlier approach or lose the sale.

No matter how affluent your prospect, there is yet another buyer "good" that you may safely introduce into your presentation. This is *savings.* Before going deeper into the subject, the reader should note that we did not intend to say or imply price. The role of price in a sale has already been touched upon and will be referred to again, but the difference between price and saving should be made clear to all who earn their living as salesmen.

By "savings," here, we mean the additional money a prospect will have because he's bought the product, and not because he's made a choice of brands. For example, a food freezer enabling the housewife to purchase food in season and store it for out-of-season use when food prices are higher represents a genuine saving. Let's consider still another example to illustrate this same point. Assuming that a person wishes to travel from one city to another, travel by bus, no matter which line he uses, is surely a saving over other modes of transportation.

Another way of looking at this matter of savings is to think in terms of presenting the sale to the prospect as an investment. "If you will buy my product, I will give you something in return that will enable you to get back more money than you've spent," the salesman, in effect, might be saying. This appeal, in a much more sophisticated form of course, could be used, for instance, with our steam-shovel prospect. Yet, as we have indicated, it is by no means confined to capital equipment sales.

In our capitalistic society, it is safe to assume that every-one can use more money than he already has. At the same time, most of us accept the fact that, to earn more money, we must spend more. Naturally, we don't wish to spend a penny more than we must, but many a prospect has bypassed the promotional, low-priced leader in a store because he has been sold on the concept of his purchase as an investment. This is especially true in these days of high cost of service, and the possibility of other high up-keep charges. Again, it is not necessary—it is even un-wise—to scare your prospect with the thought of expensive repair bills, but the aspect of savings by spending a little more now should not be overlooked by any salesman who wishes to rise above the ranks of "order-taker."

We are almost at the end of our list of possible customer "goods" that could accrue from a sale. In fact, there is just one more we could mention. After we consider an appeal to the prospect's vanity (status), love of pleasure (hedo-nism), desire for an easier life (comfort or convenience), a longer life (health), and more money (savings), the only "good" we can use is an appeal to his *senses.*

Some sales experts consider this no more than a varia-tion on the "hedonism" theme, but there is sufficient difference in intent to list it separately. Instead of buying something merely "because I deserve it," the sense buyer will tell you that it is either pleasant to look at, touch, smell, taste, or hear. These are the well-known five senses, which everyone possesses, and there is hardly a product that does not appeal to at least one of these, either directly or indirectly. If there is any doubt in the reader's mind, let him think about the colorful manner in which railroads decorate their diesel locomotives and freight boxcars these days, despite the obvious fact that these industrial items have a much more utilitarian use.

In the case of some products, such as flowers or works of art purchased for other than investment purposes, this attraction to one of the senses is the very heart of the sale. For others, the relationship is a bit more subtle. Color may be the reason why a prospect chooses one manufacturer's product over another, but in most instances the choice is made after the decision to buy has been reached. A red car may be more appealing than a black one, but before we get to that stage of the sale the prospect, hopefully, has been invited to get behind the wheel to sense the "feel" of the car. Likewise, few sales of radios or phonographs are made without at least a reference to the "sound" the prospect will enjoy. It is, of course, impossible to assign a value to such things, varying as they do in importance from one prospect to the next. But to ignore the impact of the purchase on the buyer's senses is to pretend that customers aren't human.

A direct approach to the sense appeal—such as listening to the sound, sampling the taste, etc.—is, naturally, best. However, the customer whose senses may not be so sharp as to detect the value immediately can be assisted by a psychological gambit known as "ideosensory response." The reader may recall, from an earlier chapter, how ideomotor reactions, shared by all of us, can be used to get the prospect to move in a desired manner. Ideosensory responses are quite similar except that they are suggestions for experiencing some sensual reaction rather than a physical one. If you have ever entered a room, and felt perfectly comfortable until someone called your attention to a foul odor, you know exactly what this means. To cite another example: haven't you ever been progressing very nicely on some project until a "friend" wondered aloud how you could ever work with all of that background noise? In a positive vein, a salesman can use this same principle by suggesting the clear sound, delightful aroma, home-cooking taste, or what have you of whatever it is he's selling.

Understanding why people buy, as we have been attempting to analyze in this chapter, is important. Yet, if there are just six basic "goods" that a customer can get out of a purchase—no matter what he's buying—the reader may justifiably inquire why the ratio of all sales attempted to those completed is less than ten to one. After all, isn't this just a matter of calling the prospect's attention to one or more of those benefits? The problem, unfortunately, is not so easily solved. Selling is now and probably always will remain an interpersonal relationship wherein the prospective customer's fears and prejudices, as well as what he thinks of the salesman, is often just as important as what he thinks of the product and its price. We shall devote the entire next chapter to things a salesman can do and attitudes he can assume to better this relationship. Here, though, let us turn our attention to the most important reason a customer or prospect won't buy—no matter what he thinks of the product or the salesman.

Never forget that practically every prospect you encounter is afraid. He may hide or attempt to hide this emotion, as so many do, by being overdemanding, keeping you waiting, or raising his voice, but these are "games" we've all learned to play when we're afraid, and we must never forget that customers are people. Because we doubt that we'll get a dissenting vote on that one, let's review a few of these fears with an eye toward learning how to meet them in a sales situation. Bear in mind, though, that we are not referring here to the matter of life-or-death fears, which we all share, but the specific reservations that everyone brings to a sale.

For one thing, your prospect fears your expertise at the same time that he is coming to you for advice. Sounds foolish, doesn't it? Yet consider your own feelings the last time you debated a subject with someone whose superior knowledge of the topic you had to admit. Weren't you just a little afraid? Right or wrong, your customer believes that you know more about your product line than he does. At the same time, because he knows who pays your salary, nothing can convince him that, when the chips are down, you will not place your firm's best interests above his.

Your job, therefore, is certainly not to make light of this fear. In fact, you would do well to bring it out into the open as soon as you detect the first note of hesitancy in your prospective buyer's voice. Of course you are working to make a profit for your company. On the other hand, there is much to be gained from demonstrating to the buyer that your firm's success depends, largely, upon satisfied customers. Tell him, as politely as possible, that the company will not go out of business after this one sale, and that its reputation is solidly behind the product you're selling.

Perhaps you'll discover this same fear in still another

form. Unfortunately, as a result of bitter experience, many prospects wonder if the product will look as nice or perform as well when they get it home as it did on the sales floor. This, too, is a perfectly logical fear, because nobody expects the salesman to have anything but a perfect model on display. In response to this fear, most American firms have developed one or more guarantees calculated to set the customer's mind at ease for periods ranging from ninety days to five years. These are necessarily so complicated to cover all contingencies, though, that the customer either doesn't read them or is even further frightened by the legal language of the document. (Maybe he has missed a significant point that could void the whole guarantee.)

No piece of paper will ever free you from the responsibility of reassuring the prospect that the product will be just as satisfying after the sale is consummated, but this can be accomplished in a number of ways. You can, for one, mention the names of other satisfied customers with whom the prospect may be familiar. For another, you can offer to stage an in-home demonstration *after* the sale, just to make certain that the customer is getting the maximum benefit out of the purchase. These and other solutions will come to mind, though, only after you recognize that the prospect harbors this fear.

Closely allied to the above is the buyer's fear that he may not have properly communicated to you his needs. Although he now believes that you are truly on his side, he may hesitate. "Perhaps I've overlooked something," he may tell himself. "I'd better wait until I'm sure of what I want." For many of these people, unfortunately, that moment never seems to come.

You can best meet this challenge by remembering not

to undersell your product. It is very possible that one of its benefits will awaken a need in the prospect that he didn't realize existed. If what you're selling will really perform as you claim it will, there is no danger in talking about all of its uses.

One last word about this business of fear. Quite possibly the greatest fear that most prospects have is that, after they've completed the purchase, they will look foolish either in the eyes of their spouse, their friends, or themselves. These people need the security of knowing that nobody will say, "Why did you buy that!" It's rather difficult to lay down general rules for meeting and countering this fear, because its roots may run in a number of different directions. Is the prospect afraid that, after he's made his purchase, he'll learn that he could have bought it for less elsewhere? Is he afraid that someone else will talk him out of his need for it? Does he dread discovering that, among his friends, the brand does not have the reputation you claim it has? Oh, these fears exist all right, but they are quickly dispelled by the salesman who invites the spouse to be part of the transaction, who knows what the competition is offering, and who can communicate the value of national reputation.

Chapter 6

Why They Buy from Us

Each of us knows the salesman who always seems to do the correct thing. He is right on the spot, with his presentation neatly organized, when the prospect is in a buying frame of mind. At other times he is unobtrusively "prospecting" for potential purchasers, but never with so much as a trace of desperation in his manner or voice. Observing this salesman in action, like a well-oiled piece of machinery, is a genuine pleasure. In addition to everything else that's "smooth" about him, he seems to know instinctively when to shift from weighty business talk to light chatter, the better to maintain the interest of the buyer. To summarize: this man is a real "pro."

In contrast, there is the poor soul who couldn't end up in the wrong place at the wrong time more often if he tried. His prospects never seem to have time to listen to his "pitch," and, when he does get an opportunity to talk, whatever he says seems to rub the potential customer the wrong way. You know this fellow, too: the one with more excuses for failure than orders in his pocket: the character who couldn't sell a life insurance policy to a kamikaze pilot. What makes this "loser" all the more pitiful is that he apparently studies more and tries harder than his more successful contemporaries.

Of course, the majority of us—winning some and losing others—could probably be classified somewhere between those two extremes. It's a little difficult to say exactly what constitutes a good percentage of sales "closes," so much depends upon what we're selling to whom. However, in a typical retail business, for example, sales should be made to over 50 percent of the prospects who enter the store, and 70 to 80 percent "closes" are not uncommon. These goals are worth striving for. In fact, we would be wise to set our sights on closing 100 percent of our attempted sales so that we will never be so satisfied with our performance that we fail to at least consider the advantages for change in our approach.

In this regard, the importance of analyzing the reasons for success of one salesman as compared with others in the same organization who may be selling the same product, at the same price, even to the same group of prospects, cannot be overanalyzed. Given these same sets of circumstances, how else can we explain those differences in results if we don't take into account the *personality* of the salesman? And was there ever a more overworked word?

"Personality" tests are now common in most business firms with over a handful of employees. Too, for the price of a daily newspaper, you can take one of a number of short, syndicated personality quizzes. And, in the best "Virginia Woolf" tradition, analyzing each other's personalities has become a popular husband-and-wife pastime. There is no doubt that all but a comparatively few of these "studies," those that are administered by professional psychologists, do far more harm than good. Accenting the negative in one's psychological makeup, as they do, creates only self-doubt, and is no more effective than telling a man with a broken leg to get up and walk.

Within the framework of our use of the word "personality" is the very special pattern of such things as speech, dress, behavior, and fears, which give unity and distinctiveness to one's actions. It is, we repeat, a combination of *all* of these things, and judging an individual by one of these factors alone, as do so many do-it-yourself tests, is, to say the least, grossly unfair. As this is written, for instance, the rallying cry of members of the long-haired, younger-generation "hippie" cult is that if long hair was good enough for the founding fathers of our country it is good enough for them. Forgotten in this argument is the fact that hard work, clean clothes, and good manners went along with the long hair of that day.

While there is little disagreement over the importance of personality—some call it "style"—particularly in a sales situation, there is less unanimity of opinion on how we can use this knowledge to improve sales efficiency. Some advocate the "supermarket" approach. In other words, get rid of the salesman and simply permit the customer to choose from merchandise displayed on shelves or in catalogs. Evidence of this form of "salesmanship" abounds. Traditional food supermarkets are already stocked with a variety of durable goods, ranging from household appliances to automotive accessories. However, the "sixties" have also given birth to a host of "space age" products, so technical in nature and involving such large outlays of cash, that the need for personable salesmen who speak the consumers' "language" is greater than ever. To prosper in this environment, others maintain, the salesman must adjust his personality to the times—to *empathize* with the very common feelings of insecurity, anxiety, and loneliness that are also hallmarks of our fast-moving society.

Adjusting one's personality to not only know what a prospect is thinking but how he actually "feels" about such commonplace sensations is not only good salesmanship, it is indispensable in any interpersonal relationship. Consider, for example, the case of a salesman who is selling a pain-relieving agent. How well do you imagine this man could succeed if he himself had never experienced pain? Without this empathy, which, as we noted in an earlier chapter, means sensing the same emotional response as the next person, all of the product knowledge in the world would sound quite hollow. And it is precisely this dry, "empty" talk that is the common denominator of most unsuccessful sales campaigns—no matter how technically correct they may be.

Pain, of course, is one of the easiest sensations with which to empathize. At one time or another, all of us have experienced pain. We recognize it, and know exactly how it "feels." Less obvious but equally important are those more subtle, universal emotional influences that dictate the response of a prospect. One of the best-known psychotherapists of our day, Dr. Rollo May, believes that today more people are motivated by feelings of insecurity and anxiety than by any other factor. He points out that, from the moment of the cutting of the physical umbilical cord at birth, each of us is engaged in a never-ending struggle to cut the "psychological umbilical cord" to our parents, particularly to the mother, that has always meant warmth and security. Fears and doubts of our own abilities to succeed continue to haunt us through school, vocational choice, marriage, and even right up to the moment when we face death.

Although past generations were, basically, no more secure than ours, feelings of doubt and insecurity were more easily contained. For one thing, it was inconceivable that anyone would work at anything but the most essential of jobs on Sunday—the Lord's day of rest. We can only guess how many cases of nervous exhaustion were prevented by that and the other calming influences of religion. However, with his attention diverted by such things as television and jet airplanes, man has lost touch with these important values. This, plus the flagging interest in the conventional belief in God, has placed man in the intolerable position of having no authority to which to turn for emotional leadership. Is it any wonder that he feels so insecure? It was exactly this insecurity-producing void, May tells us, which the nineteenth-century philosopher Friedrich Nietzsche predicted in his widely quoted "death of God" parable. "Whither is God?" the madman in Nietzsche's story shouts, and then himself proceeds to answer:

"I shall tell you! We have killed him—you and I! . . . yet how have we done this? . . . Who gave us the sponge to wipe away the whole horizon? What did we do when we unchained this earth from its sun? . . . Whither do we move now? Away from all the suns? Do we not fall incessantly? Backward, sideward, forward, in all directions? Is there yet any up and down? Do we not err as through an infinite naught? Do we not feel the breath of empty space? Has it not become colder? Is not night and more night coming on all the while? . . . God is dead! God remains dead! . . . and we have killed him. . . ." Here the madman became silent and looked again at his listeners: They too remained silent and looked at him. . . . "I come too early," he said then. . . . "This tremendous event is still on its way." *

It is not too difficult to find evidence of insecurity in our daily lives. Job-hopping, the high divorce rate, and the

* *The Portable Nietzsche,* The Viking Press, 1954.

fact that one out of ten hospital beds is occupied by a severely emotionally disturbed person are all signs of the times. For the salesman, though, a most important signal is the stranglehold that most people, particularly the wealthiest of them, have on money. It is axiomatic in sales circles that the more affluent accounts are the most difficult to sell—and with good reason. For each of us, money is far more than a link to physical comforts, a source of power, or a status symbol. It is a form of security against a potentially hostile world: insurance, if you will, that should all else fail, and the figurative return to the womb become impossible, we will be able to provide for ourselves. This is the same feeling of insecurity that drives many men to be so successful. Therefore we should not be surprised to find these same individuals continuing to hold fast to their wealth.

The wise salesman will empathize with this sense of insecurity. He will "feel" the importance of money to the emotional well-being of his prospects, and will do nothing to threaten that security blanket. Instead he will point out how his product can, directly or indirectly, add to that protective wall. The method, of course, will vary. In some instances a simple statement of its cost-saving features will suffice. In others, assurance of the long, useful life of the item will do the trick. It should be obvious that the objective is to reassure the prospect that, in parting with his cash, he is adding to and not diminishing his security.

The second basic motivating factor with which all salesmen should learn to empathize is *anxiety*. Its influence on the sales situation can be seen in the number of "shoppers" who go from store to store before making a decision, and the purchasing agents who never seem to be able to make up their minds even when presented with irrefutable logic for buying this or that product. To a degree, this hesitancy is good. Nobody should decide upon a purchase without getting the competitive facts, but the scores of people who end up buying an obviously inferior product after surveying the market is proof of most prospects' irrational natures. The bald truth is that few people buy with their "minds." Most act or fail to act while under the emotional influence of anxiety.

For a clearer understanding of the meaning of the word, and appreciation of the difference between anxiety and its first cousin, *worry,* the reader is invited to recall the last time he crossed a street against moving traffic. If, after reaching the middle of the street, he saw a car bearing down on him from one direction, he probably worried, albeit ever so slightly, about his ability to get safely across. Responding to this fear, his heart pounded faster to supply extra blood to his legs and his adrenal glands quickly went to work manufacturing additional muscle-stimulating chemicals—all designed to get him safely across. Such are the causes and effects of worry. On the other hand, what would be the result of the reader seeing two cars coming toward him, at once, from opposite directions? Should he run forward or back? Maybe it would be safer just to stand still and hope that both drivers avoid hitting him. This indecision in the face of a very real threat is anxiety. Lesser animals than man respond to it as if "frozen" to the ground, and frequently wind up getting hurt or killed. While humans may escape this fate, they come out of the experience more or less visibly shaken, with pains in their stomachs or heads, resulting, the psychosomatic physicians tell us, from all of those body chemicals with no useful place to go.

Anxiety in the market place may not be such a life-

or-death matter, but its symptoms are the same. The worry a prospect may experience before making up his mind to buy a product is small when compared with the anxiety he feels when confronted with a choice of similar items. There is always the chance that he will make the wrong selection. The consequences of such a mistake—as in the case of a wife spending her husband's money unwisely, or an agent making the wrong purchase for his principal—can be quite serious. For this reason, the successful salesman strives to relieve the anxiety of his prospect as early as possible in his approach to a sale. We shall have much more to say about specific methods for accomplishing this in Chapter 7 ("Qualifying" the Prospect). For the present, the reader would be wise to consider the prospects he knows, and search out the evidence of anxiety he may have failed to detect in his last attempt to "close." Even this simple exercise can be most rewarding.

One final word on this vital subject. People tend to avoid anxiety-prone individuals. They serve to remind us of all the things about which *we* are anxious. Life today is too full of these middle-of-the-street situations: Will we all be destroyed in one gigantic atomic explosion? Must we either suffer the erosion of our purchasing power through inflation or go through the depths of an economic recession? Will our favorite team win the baseball World Series? Such things, ranging from deadly threats to the not-so-serious variety, disturb us, individually, because we realize that there is little or nothing we can personally do to alter the outcome of events. It is only logical, therefore, that we should minimize the number of anxiety-laden situations in which we put ourselves. This means that the salesman himself must be as free as possible from the telltale signs of anxiety—a sweating brow, nervous moving of hands, fast talk skipping from one subject to another. Remember, that all-American hero in our favorite Western film or TV show is less remembered for his good looks or physical stamina than because he always seems to know what to do.

Strange as it may seem, another reason why people buy from one salesman in preference to another is that they are *lonely,* and some individuals seem to fill that void in the empty lives so many people lead better than others. Any doubt concerning the importance of loneliness in our lives should be quickly dispelled by news reports of "Dial-a-Listener" services recently instituted in Davenport, Iowa and at the Marble Collegiate Church in New York City. Simply by dialing an advertised number, residents in that area can find a sympathetic ear to listen to their problems, discuss personal or civic affairs, or talk about anything on the caller's mind. The volunteer service, originally started as a senior citizens project, has attracted callers from all age brackets, and the number of persons who avail themselves of the comfort of hearing a sympathetic but anonymous voice in that small city has quickly risen to over one hundred and fifty monthly.

To any observer of the American scene, this demonstration of mass loneliness is not so unusual. In his book *The Lonely Crowd,* analyst David Riesman long ago pointed out that the primary goal of this generation is to be accepted by the peer group rather than emerge, alone, at the top of the heap. This drive for acceptance, coupled with our enthusiasm for mechanical efficiency and our striving for the highest standard of living in the world, caused us to abandon thinking of the individual as anything but a rung on that ladder to "success."

This is manifest, too, in the "supermarket" concept of marketing mentioned earlier. The price we pay for reduced selling costs in these markets is dehumanization of the customer to the point where she or he is a faceless blur at the checkout counter. It all seems to fit into our "modern" way of life, in which the husband goes off to work for a gigantic corporation where he is made to feel like the small cog he is, while the wife, who is becoming increasingly involved in business herself, attempts to preserve a semblance of family life around children who can easily rush off to find their satisfaction in joining the "crowd," each member of whom is as lonely as the next.

If, into this scene, there comes a salesman who treats his customers as the individuals they are he *must* be greeted as a breath of fresh air. Even today this is not impossible. A good start can be made merely by addressing the prospect by name. (That's where a good memory is so vital.) But there are many other things a salesman can do to make it clear that he cares for the human being before him. A solicitous suggestion to "take a chair" or the offer of a cool drink on a warm day can go a long way toward establishing this personal relationship. The epitome of solicitude, however, is the example of the salesman who sends a prospect to a competitor when he realizes that he can't fully satisfy him. Perhaps, that's why they called it a "miracle on 34th Street" the day Macy's "told" Gimbels.

If you wish to perfect the closest possible kinship with people—and successful selling hinges more upon that than any other factor—it is essential that you understand the impact on others of such common emotions as we have mentioned here. There are others, of course, but mastering these is enough of a chore for individuals who have never really thought about them. The path to such better comprehension of the "feelings" of others is long and tortuous, because before you can truly appreciate the hopes, ambitions, and fears of others you must be on such intimate terms with yourself, physically and psychologically, that you can separate yourself from these same emotional bonds. Then, and only then, will you be free to manipulate these ties in yourself and others rather than be enslaved by them.

In short, we are saying that, before product knowledge or prospect list, the salesman who gets the order first knows himself. He is as free as he can be from the pressures of society without withdrawing from that society. He knows that he must work to eat, but he does not worship money. He knows that what others think of him has a direct bearing on his success or failure, but he knows too that what he thinks of himself is far more important. And, finally, he knows that, as vital as his task is to him, the world is full of people who are just as involved in whatever it is they are doing, and "fitting in" means relating his efforts to the activities of others.

If this seems like the tall order that it is, remember that the goal is not only success in selling but personal satisfaction. Isn't that worth any sacrifice? Consider the extremes to which the real leaders of the world, particularly those in the Far East, have gone to empty their minds of self-imposed distractions by foresaking worldly goods, and even their own emotions, the better to be sensitive to the "feelings" of their followers. Certainly, few people in this century have come as close to this control of self as did the great Mohandas Gandhi, who, through the exercise of his inner power, managed to "sell" the mighty British Empire on the idea of political freedom for the people of India. Describing his source of strength to carry on against great odds, and to relate to both king and commoner alike, Gandhi wrote:

Bramacharya means control of the senses in thought, word
and deed. Every day I have been realizing more and more the
necessity for restraints of the kind I have detailed above. There
is no limit to the possibilities of renunciation, even as there is
none to those of bramacharya. Such bramacharya is impossible
of attainment by limited effort. For many it must remain only
as an ideal. *An aspirant after bramacharya will always be conscious
of his shortcomings, will seek out the passions lingering in the
innermost recesses of his heart and will incessantly strive to get
rid of them.* So long as thought is not under complete control
of the will, bramacharya in its fullness is absent. Involuntary
thought is an affectation of the mind, and curbing of thought,
therefore, means curbing of the mind which is even more difficult
to curb than the wind. Nevertheless the existence of God within
makes even control of the mind possible. *Let no one think that
it is impossible because it is difficult.* It is the highest goal, and
it is no wonder that the highest effort should be necessary to
attain it.*

Of course it is difficult. Furthermore, in our modern
martini-drinking, convention-giving society, it is practically
impossible for anyone to find the time to commune with
his thoughts, let alone practice control of them. Yet this
is precisely what we must do, because an emotion learned
is an emotion mastered, while ignorance of our true feelings is still slavery. To better appreciate the significance
of this to our work, let us return to the case of the salesman
selling that pain-relieving agent. We agreed that, if this
salesman had never himself experienced pain, he would
never have much results to show for his efforts. On the
other hand, if the salesman was in pain, no matter how
slight, at the time he made his call, could we reasonably
expect him to make a maximum effort? If you've ever been
acutely aware of a pain in the neck or a bothersome hang-

The Story of My Experiments with Truth, M. K. Gandhi, Public Affairs
Press, 1948.

nail while "pitching" a prospect, you know the answer to that one.

In the example above, the reader will find an illustration of the double-edged nature of the emotional sword. It is presented here because pain, unlike other emotions such as insecurity, anxiety, or loneliness, is usually a no-nonsense type of feeling. You either have it or you don't! It is comparatively easy to recognize. Yet, no matter which emotion or sensation we're dealing with, the effect on our sales efforts are the same. Misunderstood, unrecognized, and uncontrolled in ourselves or others, such emotions and feelings can "kill" more deals than any competition. With a clear understanding of how we "feel," though, there need be no limits to our success as long as we are selling to people. And while long practice sessions are definitely indicated, the steps to follow are easy to learn.

First, you must know, without any doubt, how you "feel." The best way to accomplish this is the easiest—ask yourself! That is, find some quiet place, as free as possible from distractions, and make yourself comfortable. Then, as we learned in an earlier chapter, concentrate on the various parts of your body, one at a time, and experience the sensation of pain or comfort that comes to mind. Your feet may hurt because your shoes are too tight. Similarly, your shirt collar may be pinching your neck, and all this will keep you from your best performance in the market place, but you'll never start to know this if you don't ask your feet or neck how they feel.

With a little practice, you will master the art of recognizing physical discomforts before they can do much harm, and be ready for the more difficult step of sensing your emotions. Are you insecure because of something the boss said this morning? Perhaps you are anxious over a pending appointment with a physician, or maybe something your wife said before you left for work has left you more lonesome than usual. After you've discovered how profitable it can be to detect those easier physical problems, turn your thoughts to questions such as these. You'll learn that at this very moment your mind is experiencing some sort of emotion. It will pay you to know what it is. Are you feeling happy, sad, bored, worried, or interested? That principal thought is influencing your actions right now. That's why, whatever your emotional feelings may be, it is important that you know them well, even if you have to lock yourself in a bare room to discover them.

Second, once you know how you "feel," do something to change the sensation, if it is not in your best interests. This is not too difficult, once you know exactly what you wish to change, once you refuse to settle for vague feelings of uneasiness. In these days of modern medicine (aspirin, etc.) pain may be the simplest sensation to control, but mastery of the others, after recognizing them, is no less possible. The key here is always to remember that you have a choice—at least in this democratic-oriented society you do. If another's actions bother you, you can either say so and attempt to get him to mend his ways; or you may simply walk away to find someone more compatible; or, in the final analysis, you may elect to "grin and bear it," because you are after bigger game, worth far more than this petty annoyance. If that's the situation in which you find yourself, surveying the alternatives will make the right path most evident.

Third, and this step can be taken only after the first two have been thoroughly mastered, you must learn to accept the fact that others (among them, all of your prospects) carry these same emotional burdens. For instance, they, too, may suffer from some vague physical discomfort—not serious enough to demand attention but so distracting as to impair their judgment. Their reaction to you may well be influenced by what has happened to them long before you appeared on the scene. Only a skilled analyst could tell just how strong these "other" influences may be. It is not our job here to psychoanalyze your prospects. Yet many of their unfavorable responses, resulting from things over which you have no control, can be negated by the way you conduct yourself, and your ability to "be yourself" rather than react to the way they feel.

To summarize, it is foolhardy to look for escape from the real world with all of its negative influences—the morning quarrel with the spouse, the gruff behavior of a friend, the remarks of an impertinent salesclerk—on both seller and buyer. Your objective, though, should be to rise above such happenings—by understanding yourself and them so well that you will maintain your freedom "to be yourself" and not react to these annoyances. Then, fortified with this inner strength, behave in such a manner as to assist others in setting down the same heavy load we all carry. At least don't add to it. In this direction lies the most profitable of human relationships. Perhaps a few examples from common sales experiences will serve to cement the message.

Is there a reader who has not, at least once in his career, been forced to face an angry prospect? Maybe someone whose last order was so badly handled by the shipping department that he has threatened never again to do business with the company. It is even likely that the very thought of making this call stirred within the salesman angry emotions of his own over what he considered the injustice of the prospect's feelings. "He can't expect me personally to ship the merchandise, too," the salesman may think. "Doesn't he know that good warehouse help is hard to get these days? Wait a minute—if he imagines that he's going to use this as an excuse to take his business to some friend or relative, he's got another think coming!"

Does the above sound familiar? It's a safe bet that the resulting confrontation between salesman and buyer went in either one of two directions. If the salesman failed to recognize the path down which his prospect's and his own anger was carrying him, some heated words were exchanged and a sale was lost. However, if our hero coolly calculated that his task was to make sales and not win arguments, he adjusted his approach to mollify the customer and went on to close the deal. "You're absolutely right!" he may have stated. "Our entire industry is suffering from an acute shortage of competent shipping room help. That's why we're instituting a training program for high school dropouts. Meanwhile, we've assigned one of our executives the task of seeing to it that all orders are properly filled. Your next order, for instance . . ."

In another vein, we recall covering two adjacent territories with two equally technically-qualified, hardworking salesmen.

The first rushed off before breakfast each morning to make his initial call. If he could get there before his competition, he reasoned, he would be better able to "load" his customer with what he was selling so that there would be little left to spend for competitive merchandise, no matter how attractive the value. That little pang of hunger could wait until the more important business was concluded. The only trouble was that, obviously, he could only call on one prospect first. Therefore, to be ahead of other salesmen as much as possible, he maintained that pace through lunch time, then throughout the day. The reader will now easily recognize that this man spent all of his time *reacting* to an uncontrollable situation. Then, tired and hungry, but uncomplaining because he was too busy to recognize the symptoms, this salesman gulped down a late dinner, muttering all the while about the erratic performance of his accounts.

The second fellow started work after breakfast. He had a definite plan of *action* built around the buying habits and location of his prospects. Sure, he'd lose a couple of sales to salesmen who got to these customers first. But he viewed his job as a long-time career, and if he didn't sell them this trip he left enough good will to insure his welcome the next time around. This man took his "break," not at a specific time, but when he sensed that he was getting tired and hungry. At the end of a day of comparative smooth performance, he settled back to a quiet dinner and contemplation of the personal and business world in which he moved. Is it any wonder that the commissions of the second salesman greatly exceeded those of the first?

It is doubtful that, true as they are, these basic personality differences will ever be cited by a customer for buying from one salesman in preference to another. They are more important for the seller to study so that he can improve his "image," or the personality he projects to his prospects. This mental picture is seldom painted with words such as "adjusted" or "mature"—the result of knowing ourselves so well. Instead, unless they are psychologically oriented, people will say that their favorite salesman is "pleasant," "comfortable to be with," or "knowledgeable." Don't you feel that way about your contact at the place where you prefer to shop? Your customers, of course, are no different. Therefore, any consideration of why they buy from us would not be complete without considering the role these stated, not-so-superficial reasons play in the buying decision.

The *pleasant* fellow is not, necessarily, the one who is always smiling, although that expression can go a long way towards setting a prospect at ease. More important is the fact that this individual is *uncomplaining*. It seems that the hardest thing for most of us to learn is that nobody loves an invalid—physical or emotional. If this seems cruel, remember that practically everyone is carrying some sort of burden. The problems of these prospects, no matter how slight they may seem to you, are heavy enough to them without having to be reminded constantly of the troubles of others. We may wish it to be otherwise, but this is the way people are. For a limited while they may listen sympathetically to your complaints of marital difficulties, trouble with your boss, a headache, or a delivery of merchandise you could have sold them had it arrived on time. Yet if this continues for a sustained period they will tire of being reminded of difficulties they may someday encounter for themselves (another example of the negative effects of anxiety). Therefore, the success of salesmen who are really handicapped—and there are many of them—is due to their being so proficient in other ways that their customers are unaware of the burdens they are carrying.

Comfortable people are only slightly more difficult to define. Ours is truly a society composed of many subcultures. Our customers probably come from many different religious or ethnic backgrounds. Because they are so accustomed to it, they are comfortable in this environment with its peculiar mannerisms, speech, dress, etc. Their attitude toward people and things is dictated less by mature judgment and more by the total of their experiences—another thing over which the salesman has no control. On the other hand, he can and should make every effort possible to put his prospects at ease. We will also elaborate on this in the next chapter, but now let us consider some of the comfort-giving things that generally apply to prospects, no matter what their life style may be.

Take your physical appearance, for example. While some people profess to admire the uninhibited style of those who permit their hair to grow long and wear ill-fitting clothes, others are offended by these same things. (It is not for us to choose sides in this issue.) However, the well-groomed person who does not flaunt his appearance is judged by what he really is and does. Subconsciously, we skip from his dress to other more important facets of his personality. Is it, therefore, worth the risk of offending with our appearance? We think not. At the same time, dress can be positively used to set a prospect at ease. We know of one appliance store, for instance, that dresses its salesmen in service technicians' uniforms. The goal, obviously, is to make the customer feel that she is dealing with an expert. This type of assurance is just what the customer needs to make her feel comfortable buying a complicated product of which she may be technically ignorant.

Another way that you can make prospects feel comfortable in your presence is to scale your "pitch" *up* to their level. We say "up," because the worst sin you can commit here is to talk *down* to people. All of us fancy ourselves experts. We seldom admit, even to ourselves, the many things we don't know. That's why the salesman who treats his prospects as the experts they think they are is bound to have the greater number of customers. Naturally, this can be overdone. We can presuppose so much knowledge on the part of the prospect that we fail to mention the very features that could clinch the sale. The idea is to walk the very fine line between a friendly discussion of a product or service and a pedantic lecture, to say something about a feature and then look for clues in the prospect's reaction that tell us to press further with this point. In this way, many customers who say little if anything are made to feel at ease.

Most salesmen who call on prospects make it a point to know the name of the buyer and something about the business of the company before they enter the purchasing agent's office. That's just good common sense, but it is not enough to portray the salesman as the *knowledgeable* person he is. It is also a little difficult for the salesman to know much more than the prospect's name when he comes in the store. There is just no way of knowing much about the business of a person who walks through that retail doorway.

For all of the above-mentioned reasons, the successful salesperson never completes his education. Naturally, he is always learning all that he can about the features of whatever it is he's selling. In addition, though, he keeps abreast of trade developments so that, even if he fails to make a sale to an industrial prospect, he can leave some precious gem of information that will linger as a better calling card long after he's gone. You may be certain that, depending upon the value of his information, he'll be warmly greeted the next time he calls. The retail salesman who wishes to be similarly welcomed will learn all that he can about local civic affairs, whether they be zoning laws, school board, or tax issues. It is not necessary, it is even dangerous, to take sides in such matters, but even objective intelligent analysis must be based on knowledge. Once again we are reminded that our customers are hungry for much more than product information. The salesman who is in a position to impart this knowledge is building a relationship that transcends the immediate sale. And aren't we all just as concerned with tomorrow's business?

In this chapter, we have tackled the very difficult subject of customers' preference for the personality of one salesman over another; why some retail shoppers consistently ask for a certain salesman by name; why some industrial salesmen never seem to have difficulty in catching the buyer's ear. Admittedly, were we to ask individuals why they like this person better than another, the answers would be so broad that they would be impossible to categorize. Yet the preference does exist; we cannot afford to ignore that fact. To get a firm grasp on the subject, a salesman need not be a psychoanalyst. Much headway can be made by dividing the reactions of our prospects to personality into two groups: those which are stated, and those equally important but subconscious motives which draw people together or apart.

The failure of many individuals who engage in the business of selling to sit down and look quietly at their prospects and themselves in this light has led to much unnecessary frustration. Too many misguided salesmen have purchased books or taken courses calculated to lead to instant success in selling only to discover that in practice the lessons simply don't work. Even worthwhile exercises in understanding "buyer psychology" turn out to be impractical in the market place if they are not accompanied by a study of "self."

At this point, perhaps, we should offer our apologies to the reader if he purchased this volume expecting to mine such shortcuts to fame and fortune. Our intention, as we stated at the very beginning, is to present thought-starting suggestions to the ambitious salesperson in the hope that he will be encouraged to pursue the lengthy introspection, or closer look into one's motives, and practice so vital to being a better person and a better salesman.

Chapter 7

"Qualifying" the Prospect

You are alone on the sales floor. You are a trifle worried, because business has been somewhat less than spectacular all day long, but suddenly your outlook is brightened. Not one, but two prospects enter the store almost simultaneously. The first walks over to one of your attractive displays featuring a deluxe model. She fingers it lovingly, is obviously interested in learning more about it. She may even look at you questioningly. Meanwhile, the second prospect stands, hesitatingly, just inside the doorway. She seems lost in this environment, but has apparently come into the store for something. Assuming, furthermore, that both prospects also display a degree of impatience, which do you approach first? What do you say to hold her attention, while you try to point the second one toward a sale, if, indeed, this is the tactic you should follow? How can you best be certain that you are not devoting too much time to a prospect who is "just shopping"?

Then again, you may be at the end of a hot, tiring day of beating the bushes for outside customers. There is just time to make one more call, but you have two prospects in the same neighborhood. The first, your background file cards tell you, is a cantankerous old body who has purchased from you before, but never lets you get out of his office without belittling your efforts and making you feel that he is doing you a favor by buying from you. Nevertheless, this customer is just about due for a reorder. The second is really a "cold" prospect, except that the lead has been passed along to you by a fellow salesman whose opinions you respect. "This guy needs what you're selling," your friend has told you. "Besides," he adds, "he is a happy-go-lucky, intelligent person who makes you feel good even when he says no." On which prospect do you spend your remaining minutes in the day? If it's the first, how do you know which models to dwell upon so that you can stick to business, and save yourself as much as possible from a senseless tongue-lashing? What does this customer really want from you? If you choose the prospect who has never bought from you before, in what order do you present your line to be positive that you make the best possible sale? He may be pleasant to be with, but you want his business. How do you start getting it?

The process by which you, as a salesman, make decisions of that sort is known as "qualifying" the prospect. Whether they do this consciously, in some step-by-step order, or not, all salesmen go through the business of qualifying a prospect sometime before the close of a sale. They attempt to determine, first of all, whether they are confronted with someone who is prepared to buy *now*, or whether they are talking with an individual who is merely "sounding out" the market, either as a professional shopper or with intentions to buy at a later date.

Then, after determining that he has a "live" prospect on his hands, the salesman will make some effort to distinguish between what the prospective customer says he wants and what he really needs—and, just as important, if he can really afford to pay for it. Last, but far from least, "qualifying" should turn up the one appeal to that prospect that has the best chance of turning him into a customer. Sometimes these steps involve no more than a direct question or two. At other times they require lengthy, involved probing. The goal, though, is always the same—to save the salesman's precious time, point him in the right direction for a close, and establish the best possible communications link between prospect and salesman.

One of the most succinct yet descriptive stories of qualification around is the now-classic tale, attributed to Bernard Shaw, of a conversation with a wealthy, aristocratic woman. "Would you go to bed with me for a million dollars?" Shaw supposedly asked.

"Yes, I guess so," the woman replied.

"Would you do it for half a million?" the literary wit then inquired.

"Yes, I suppose so."

"Well then, how about ten dollars?"

At this, the woman was said to have drawn back, haughtily, and exclaimed: "What do you think I am!"

"Madam," Shaw replied, "we've already determined that. Now, we're merely trying to establish the price."

Unfortunately, the business of qualifying prospects in most legitimate businesses is not so easy. One of the chief stumbling blocks is that the customer is seldom positive about what she or he wants. More common, by far, is the prospect who comes into a showroom asking for something such as "an automobile." Very likely he's been attracted by a low-priced, advertised model. He may even have a good idea of the body style and color he prefers, but he's much less positive about the size of the engine or the accessories he would like on his car. That's where "qualifying" comes in, and it starts the moment the salesman hears of the prospect.

Unless we are selling in a multidepartment store, it is safe to assume that each person coming through our doorway is seeking something in the specialty nature of our product. (In a department store, prospects have a way of qualifying themselves by going to a certain department.) Of course, the salesman who goes house to house on "cold canvas" calls has the most difficult qualifying job of all, but, as we shall soon discover, by asking the right questions even he can learn much about what is on the mind of his prospect. As a rule, though, retailers make it simple for the shopper to signify his initial interests by advertising and decorating their stores in a certain manner. We identify a barber shop with a striped pole, a drug store with apothecary jars, etc. At least the name of the firm and/or its window display of merchandise tell the prospect at a glance what type of products or services he can expect to find inside. As a matter of fact, the public is so conditioned to this sort of advertising that, were we to put a barber pole outside a funeral parlor, some character would eventually come in for a haircut.

One way or another, then, we have a confrontation of the prospective buyer with the seller. "How do you do?" the seller all-too-often begins. "May I help you?" Our hero has, unintentionally, "blown" his first opportunity for further qualifying the prospect by asking the right question in the wrong way. He would have done as well, if not better, by walking up to the shopper with a smile on his face, but saying nothing. That would have given the prospect an opportunity to make a declarative statement of his wishes. "I'm interested in a color television set," "May I use your rest room?" etc.

The "may I help you?" approach went out of style long

ago, and with good reason. In semantic circles, the question is known as a "closed end" one. In other words: it gives the party at the other end an opportunity to terminate the conversation then and there merely by saying "no," leaving the one who asked the question with his bare face hanging out. Even if the prospect says "yes," the salesman is not much better off. He knows nothing more about the individual facing him, and he must carry the ball again with still another question. The real "pros" in this business would never dream of boxing themselves in a corner in this manner. If they can think of nothing else, they may say, "*How* may I help you?" As opposed to the first, this is an "open end" question, because it calls for more than a yes or no answer, and brings forth exactly the kind of information the salesman needs to go ahead and close the sale.

It would be a grave mistake to view the opening, qualifying question as an attempt to entrap the prospect. Nobody likes to be tricked into buying anything, and the selling profession has labored too long and hard to get out from under the carnival huckster connotation to slide back into it now. We must also remember (see Chapter 6) that one of our primary objectives is to make the customer feel comfortable in our presence. As we mentioned earlier, this is fairly easy to accomplish in a physical sense. Offering a chair, a cigarette, or a hot or cold drink will do the job nicely. At the psychological level, the problem is complicated by the fact that we just can't afford the time to study the prospect's background. Nevertheless, there are some emotionally-laden words we can use and others we should avoid in our qualifying questions to establish the best rapport with the prospect.

For instance, words we should avoid as much as possible, at least in our opening remarks, would include:

Price—"value" is much better and truer.

Dirty—next time, try "soiled."

Impossible—nothing is "impossible" to an expert.

Can't—maybe you really "can't," but the prospect will feel better knowing that you tried.

Cheaper—perhaps the value is not the same, but there is nothing in your line that is "cheap."

Excuse—prospects, you will recall, have their own problems. It is better by far to tell them what you will do rather than why you didn't.

Maybe—indecision is most unbecoming in a professional. What would you think of a dentist who said: "Maybe that tooth has to come out."

Afraid—better to let sleeping fears lie.

Out of the question—see "can't."

Late—only the other fellow is late. We were "detained" by a most worthwhile mission.

We will have much more to say about the positive and negative impact of words on customers in subsequent chapters. For the present, though, you can probably add to the above list, if you will just review your own vocabulary. Merely say the word aloud and ask yourself what image is conjured up in your mind by its sound. You'll be amazed at how uncomfortable you can be with words you've been using for a lifetime.

Well, we've got the salesman and prospect together, and established that a potential sale exists—all without making the prospect ill at ease. Before proceeding further with the process of qualification, it would pay to dwell an additional moment on those cultural differences which could affect that relationship. Take time, for example. In his excellent book, *The Silent Language,** Edward T. Hall points out that in the eastern United States there are eight time "sets," or yardsticks, that are generally related to business ap-

*Doubleday & Company, Inc., 1959.

pointments: on time, five, ten, fifteen, twenty, thirty, forty-five minutes, and one hour early or late. In support of this, the reader has undoubtedly noticed how most advertised real estate properties are just "twenty minutes" from the center of town. Then, too, no matter how crowded a restaurant may be, there seldom is more than a "ten-minute" wait. Of course the real times may be longer than those, but there seems to be something enticing to the eastern American about not driving more than twenty minutes nor waiting longer than ten.

In our culture, these "sets" are extremely important, too, because they tell us much about the importance we attach to a meeting. When we say, "I can give you five minutes of my time," the impression left is entirely different from "Let's take an hour to talk it over." Even though more may be accomplished in the shorter meeting, we find it necessary to apologize for its brevity, and leave the feeling that we don't consider it important enough to warrant more time. A salesman can profit much, therefore, from the way he makes and keeps his appointments, and can better qualify his prospect by the time allotted for the purchase. It matters little whether or not the prospect has "read the book." His notions of time are a part of his cultural heritage, which, for all practical purposes, is as unchangeable as the color of his eyes.

Hall notes also that the American culture is characteristically *monochronic.* This means that we believe that the road to efficiency lies in doing one thing at a time, whether it be settling family accounts or waiting on prospects. From our earliest childhood we have been taught that the best way to solve a big problem such as too many customers for a limited sales force is to break it up into its component parts, and concentrate on them singularly. This is not to find fault with that type of thinking. It is merely to recognize it as something indigenous to our culture so that we won't be too surprised when a prospect with a Latin American background, for instance, insists upon our serving her along with someone who was there first.

Furthermore, being peculiarly American, most prospects refuse to believe that a salesman can be busy unless they see him engaged in some purely physical activity such as rearranging boxes on a shelf. It requires a great deal of practice for a salesman to do and say nothing while his customer decides upon a color. We mistakenly interpret silence as a signal for us to again assume the initiative. The reader can well imagine how such an attitude can easily conflict with a foreign culture. A Mediterranean Arab, for example, has no more than three time "sets": no time at all, now, and forever—the last being synonymous with "too long." His milieu makes no distinction between waiting a long time and a very long time.

Differences such as those already mentioned in the way each of us thinks of time can be either detrimental to the interpersonal relationship, if we fail to account for the other person's point of view, or beneficial, if we weave our sales story around the individual characteristics. Yes, we know that this is further evidence of the desirability of empathy, but the reader has already been prepared for the importance we attach to "getting over to the customer's side of the sales counter." Yet another cultural gap that must be bridged, and that is pointed out by Hall, is the attitude of people toward space—not as in interplanetary travel, but right here on Earth.

In this country, Hall observes, we tend to treat space as a sacred right, as evidence of acceptance or rejection, and as an important rung on that ladder to success. In the typical business firm, space is allotted to individuals along the walls of the office, with higher ranking executives getting the choice window positions, and the center reserved for secretarial "pools," group meetings, or some other common use. In contrast, the French and other Europeans position the boss or manager in the center, where he can keep an eye on all employees without leaving his desk. However, the significance we attach to space and the differences in outlook extend far beyond the office walls.

For example, a man can be expected to fight not only to protect his home from intruders, but also to preserve his place in line at a theater ticket window or butcher shop. Therefore, most American lines tend to be orderly affairs, in keeping with our concept of equality, with the first person to arrive at the head of the line and so on back to the last person. The aggressive individual who "crashes" the line is viewed with disdain, and, if he does this habitually, he is ostracized by the community. While we may consider this to be highly democratic and efficient, to many a foreign visitor it is evidence of our "sheeplike" nature. In his country, he will tell you, people never permit themselves to be regimented in this manner, and he must at least be understood if he carries this cultural pattern with him.

Variations on the space theme can also be seen in the distances normally kept between two individuals in conversation—in our case, a buyer and seller. Although we like to think of ourselves as the friendliest of people, here, except for the most intimate relationships, we tend to keep a distance of two or three feet between ourselves and the party with whom we're speaking. People who normally stand closer than that make us feel uncomfortable, and we qualify them as "pushy." As these persons push in on us, we find ourselves instinctively moving backward, disliking every moment of the experience. Unfortunately for better understanding among all people, the speaking distance habits of, let us say, a Latin American are quite different. He will be unable to talk comfortably unless he stands at a distance that evokes either sexual or hostile feelings in a North American. The danger is that, unaware of these cultural variations, we may qualify the foreigner as if he was raised with our backgrounds.

Better understanding is, of course, good business. Just as we must make every effort fully to understand the personality differences in our prospects, we should learn to comprehend the distinction between what they say they want and what they really need. There is a dissimilarity, you know. When we get right down to it, the real "needs" of any individual are few in number. To the overriding one of security mentioned in the last chapter, we can only add the three basic physical ones of food, clothing, and shelter. As recently as the middle of the last century, the average citizen was fortunate if he satisfied all of those needs. But, as any student of the American economy knows, times have indeed changed. Our typical buyer today consumes twice as much as he did sixty years ago, and although we have failed to eliminate poverty from the land, the vast majority of us own far more things (as much as 25 percent of our total possessions, some experts tell us) than we need for our physical well-being. And these luxuries, once sampled, quickly become necessities. It is all very much like men being perfectly satisfied to see with two good eyes. Yet, should a creature be born with an additional eye at the back of his head, and should he then lose the sight of that extra eye, he would quickly complain about his blindness.

The things we "need" today are not much different from that third eye. We have grown so accustomed to a machine for transportation and another for keeping our food cold that automobiles and refrigerators are essential to the contentment of practically every American home. Central heating and air-conditioning are also part of the new necessities of life, despite the fact that they are still considered luxuries in most parts of the world. The list of such items is practically endless, apparently limited only by the capacity of our mass production methods and the ingenuity of our advertising agencies. It is a fact, for instance, that practically every American household already has a refrigerator (100 percent saturation, the industry calls it). Still, our existing plant capacity, operating on a normal forty-hour work week, can turn out one-fourth again as many refrigerators as those which will fail beyond repair this year. Is it any wonder that we maintain the pressure on engineers and sales forces alike to add to the consuming public's list of needs?

It should be apparent, therefore, that when a potential customer speaks or thinks of those things he absolutely must have he is visualizing far more than is necessary to keep skin and bones together. He now "needs" a vacation at least once a year, a convenient news source that predigests events of the day and spits out only the essentials, comfortable transportation, a home entertainment device or two, a machine to wash his clothes and another to do his dishes, an automatic heating device and one for cooling, as well as a box to keep food fresh and cold—just as surely as his ancestors needed fire, a pure water source, the skin of a fur-bearing animal, a cave, and some grain. Nor is this expansion of needs completed. It has been estimated that the average consumer in this country will have to increase his overall consumption by as much as 50 percent in the next decade or else our assembly-line economy will falter.

The salesman who keeps abreast of the changing pattern in prospects' needs has a tremendous advantage over his less alert competitors. However, it would be an oversimplification to state that the requirements of individual consumers increase at the same rate. As we have already noted, there is, first of all, the matter of life style. To a hardworking executive, a vacation may be as much of a need as a coal-burning stove is to a slum dweller. Then there are such personal factors as age, background, place of residence, size of family, education, and current living standards, which influence our consideration of anything as a necessity. The problem becomes even more complicated when we think of the number of subdivisions within each of those groups. Any two young men will probably tell you that a car is a necessity these days, but the family man with a couple of children will have something entirely different in mind from his unmarried contemporary. That's one reason why there are so many different automobile models on the market.

Although much has been written about the American habit of buying more than we can afford, as prospects we do tend to buy according to our needs, or what we think we "must" have. No matter how far we have progressed from our caveman days, these needs are practically always physical in nature; i.e., the housewife "needs" a new dishwasher, new clothes for herself, a new sofa. It's a rare prospect, however, who expresses her "needs" in that manner. Today's educated, sophisticated shopper knows or thinks she knows exactly what she "wants"—i.e. a portable dishwasher with a hardwood top, a size ten cocktail dress in navy blue, a Danish modern sofa. That should make the salesman's job easier, but only if the salesman, through skillful questioning, listening, and observing, has determined that the prospect's needs equal her wants, that her kitchen is large enough to accommodate the dishwasher, that the size ten will really fit, that the Danish-modern styling will blend with the other furniture. That's qualifying!

We can also never be positive that the prospect is telling us his true needs. Certainly the person who enters a retail establishment or the purchasing agent who sends for a salesman has a good notion of what he wants. If he has been attracted by an advertisement, he may very well desire the item being promoted. Stimulation of this desire is, after all, the target for most advertising. Yet a shopper may be attracted by an ad or display of an automobile priced much too high for his wallet. Nevertheless, "it is a good-looking car," and "we want an automobile anyway," so "what's the harm in looking?" In many more cases than the reader may realize, the prospect will never mention that he is really in the market for something less expensive, unless the salesman broaches the subject. Rather than admit that he can't afford to buy the one featured, he will get his vicarious satisfaction in just looking—and taking up the salesman's time—and departing with his limited funds unspent.

More frequently, of course, we encounter just the opposite situation. "Loss leader" type advertising is so common in our competitive market place that we have been compelled to pass laws to protect consumers against firms that promote products they have no intention of selling, and cannot in fact even deliver. The objective, of course, is to "bait" the prospect with such an ad, and then "switch" him to a more expensive model once he's within hearing distance of the salesman's velvet-smooth voice. This sort of practice must lie heavy on the conscience of every honest salesman.

There are many reputable firms, though, that are perfectly able if not so willing to sell their low-priced, advertised models. Although a prospect might be thus attracted to the establishment, he may really want something with more features, and figure that the price of what he desires will be similarly low. Yet there is better than an even chance that he'll never mention this unless he's prodded. Remember that the prospect thinks of the salesman as an expert or else he doesn't shop the firm at all. If the expert doesn't think enough of those extra features to mention them, maybe he was wrong in wanting them in the first place.

From all of this it should be obvious that the process of qualifying a prospect as to his wants and needs is really a three-step affair. First we encounter what our potential customer says he wants. It is important that we listen carefully, and remain alert for minimal cues at this stage of the negotiations. If it's a husband and wife shopping team, for instance, he may be talking about one model while she's looking at another. Second, we must determine what the buyer *truly* needs, and never settle for what he says he wants. This is the most critical step of all, because, assuming our ability to fulfill those real needs in every way, a sale is virtually assured. Last, but very far from least, is unearthing the honest-to-goodness needs of our prospect. If, as is often the case, these differ from his wants, we must, diplomatically, get him to want what he needs. Many a salesman has made a sale but lost a repeat customer by catering only to the buyer's wants. If a mistake in judgment has been made, and the product, after it's been purchased and delivered, doesn't satisfy the need, you can safely bet your next commission check that the salesman will be blamed, and, if possible, the merchandise returned.

Some salesmen, albeit very few of them, seem to have a knack for separating their customers' needs from what they say they want without exchanging a word. Almost instinctively they go to the right rack, drawer, floor model, or catalog page. More often than not, this is the result of an in-depth knowledge of the market, plus an extreme sensitivity to "little things," such as where the buyer's eyes fall, the newspaper advertisement under his arm or on his desk, and whether or not he's brought his wife along, or, if it is an industrial sale, the other executives present besides the purchasing agent.

Yet, as important as these and other minimal cues referred to earlier may be, there is absolutely no better way to qualify a prospect's needs than to ask questions. Sometimes, of course, between asking questions and talking about our product, we tend to overdo it. Maybe that's why salesmen have the reputation for being such "gabby" fellows, but, if you'll remember to listen intelligently for the answers, pleasantly asked direct questions will help to bridge that empathy gap with your customers. And remember to keep the questions simple. Obviously they will vary depending upon what you're selling, but here are a few that can get you started thinking in the right direction.

If you're selling furniture, for example, there's absolutely nothing wrong in your asking: "In which room of your home are you planning to use this?" Then, naturally, you'll want to inquire: "What is the style of the furniture you already have?" Notice that our questions imply assuming nothing about the prospect, and, insofar as possible, we make them "open-ended." This permits our customer to swing easily into a discussion of her tastes, and, as we stated, bring her needs closer to the surface of the conversation.

No matter what your product may be, if it's a replacement sale you are far ahead of competition if you ask: "How old is your present _____?" Or, whether this is a "first" or "repeat" purchase for your prospect, you can do worse than raise the question: "Are you planning to use this regularly or for a special occasion (or job)?" The answer to the first will give you a good idea, without committing yourself, of how much wear or use the customer expects out of the product; and the second pinpoints a profitable direction for the balance of your sales story.

Most household products should never be sold before the salesman gets an answer to the question: "How large is your family?" In the first place, what with the number of different capacity units on the market, the response establishes the need quickly and pleasantly. Second, most people enjoy talking about their families. It may even give the proud parents an opportunity to brag a bit about the offspring, and, if he too is a family man, the salesman can easily make the point that he fully knows the meaning of such responsibility. That never did hurt a sale!

Get the idea? Just keep asking and listening, and you can't fail to move closer to a "close," but you still have some distance to go after you and your prospect both know what he needs, and you've determined that you have just the product or service to fill that need. Very few deals are consummated at this point. More sales have been permanently lost to half-qualified customers than to those who were not qualified at all. In the latter instance, at least, the prospective customer would be so unsure of himself that he probably wouldn't buy two ten-dollar bills for a five if J. Edgar Hoover was the salesman *without asking more questions himself.*

Your unfinished job is to determine your prospect's *order of goods.* This is just another way of asking: "How important, Mr. Customer, is that need to you?" Unfortunately, you can't always come right out and ask it, because the answer may involve some private emotional reasoning by the customer, but it is something that every salesman discovers, one way or another, before he is too long into a sale. The reader may recall that, in Chapter 4, we defined a "sale" as "an exchange of a good for a good," and we noted that, insofar as the prospect is concerned, a "good" can be many things from money to comfort. It is equally true that each of us considers all of these things "good" to a degree, but there are surely some we value more than others. For example, it is undeniably pleasant to see and touch a luxurious fabric, but you would not attempt to sell a fancy lace pillow to a hod carrier! It is safe to assume that the sensual pleasure of that pillow would be low on his scale of "goods." Yet it could be quite disastrous to assume much more than that.

Milady may need a new hat, but who is to say, just by looking at her, that she needs it to lift her spirits, keep her hair in place, or to complete an outfit planned for a special occasion? And where does price figure in her thinking? Obviously all of these things, or at least two of them, may be going through her mind when she enters the shop, but undoubtedly one is more important than the rest. Yet there is better than an even chance that, unless he *asks* the correct questions, the salesman will never know what that "hot button" is, and may waste valuable time trying to sell her the most "practical" item in the store when she's really looking for something more colorful, even if she can only use it once in a while. Here we also encounter the added difficulty of the customer not always being consciously aware of the true reason why she is in the market. We might add that this applies as much to men who buy business machines as it does to women who buy hats.

You can see that this business of qualifying the order of "goods" can get quite complicated. It is not impossible, though. Remember, your prospect is always, mentally, weighing what he can expect from the purchase against what he is paying or sacrificing for it. The decision to buy is made when the scales are finally tipped in favor of what you are offering. Qualifying the potential customer, the better to enumerate the features of the product important to him, will hasten the moment when he can no longer argue with himself, and the sale is made.

Despite the fact that tact is definitely called for, you will find it advantageous to keep your questions and statements here brief and to the point. Perhaps your customer won't come straight out and admit that he cannot afford to pay the price, and may be offended if you ask him, but he can't take offense, and you can learn much, if you ask: "Have you seen a better value than this at _____ dollars?"

Offering a choice is always a good way of getting the prospect to further qualify himself. Among other things, a choice assists him in making up his mind. If both of you are uncertain of the price he is willing to pay, for example, you can quickly put price in its true perspective by inquiring: "Are you looking for something less expensive, or the best value in a longer-lasting item?" It is entirely possible that, if it's a one-shot purchase, the customer will choose the former. Don't forget that our task is to assume nothing. Then, too, the answer to:"Is this for your living room or den?" can greatly narrow the field of items under consideration. Your prospect will appreciate the help, and you can use the time saved elsewhere.

Finally, it is imperative that you qualify your potential customer as to his fears. We have already stated that fear, no matter how slight, is an experience common to everyone who has ever purchased anything. Among some marketing experts, this may be referred to as "uncertainty"—"fear" being too much of an emotionally laden word—but it is, nonetheless, an inhibiting factor to any sale. At the same time it is important to the salesman's role, because the epitome of a fearless customer is one who orders by mail or over the phone, and we're surely not ready to admit that our jobs can be adequately filled by an "order-taker."

If fear plays such a vital part in the sales transaction, we must know more about it—specifically, the value that the customer places on it. Very likely the reader is already familiar with the prospect who is afraid of buying an item that will not truly fill his need. This is the most common of all. However, where the fear of buying the wrong thing ranks in comparison with others—overpaying, looking ridiculous in the eyes of a spouse or friends, etc.—will vary from one customer to the next. Obviously, too, it will depend upon the value to the prospect of the "good" being traded. In any case, your job is not completed until you have ferreted out these fears, and, after arranging them in order, have quelled them—one by one.

Once again, the procedure is exactly the same as it is for any other type of qualification—ask questions! In the process, though, you will have the opportunity to learn much more about your prospect than the things he fears. "Have you purchased from us before?" can elicit information vital to the credit department, an opinion of your firm's service, and even some knowledge of the customer's taste, in addition to how much confidence he has in the company.

This business of piggybacking on one question is a good time-saver, and should not be overlooked. If, for instance, there is a note of hesitancy in the caller's voice ("My God, what will my wife think!" may be the unspoken expression), you can turn this to advantage in putting him at ease and in solidifying an appointment by asking: "Would it be more convenient for you if I called tonight or tomorrow evening?" Much the same multiplicity of information can result from: "On which side of town is your home located?"

Dealing with fear can be a very tricky routine. We certainly don't wish to spark any concern that may not be present. This is the best reason for never using such words as "fear" or "afraid." Other things to avoid are tales of poor experiences others may have had with the product—no matter how much they were eventually satisfied or whose fault it was—and even a hint that this is the "last" item of its kind in stock. If it is really such a "hot" mover, you won't have trouble selling it elsewhere, and, if it is not, why raise the question of why it has not been sold before this?

There are times, we recognize, when fear itself is the best way to motivate a prospect. Some products or services, such as burglar alarms, cater to fear, but it should be obvious that the customer buys such things from companies and salesmen in whom he has the utmost confidence. Many a dishwasher has been sold through that advertising theme "wash dishes in water hotter than you would put your hands," which is another way of saying "protect yourself from germs." You may be certain, however, that the salesman who closed the sale was a germ-free-looking fellow who knew how to use fear as the ally it can be.

Chapter 8

The Vital
Role of
Demonstrations

Fortunate indeed is the salesman who has an easily demonstrable product to sell. Literally, putting it and a prospect together is much easier for him than for those of his contemporaries who must rely upon word power alone. Given the option between "showing" and "telling," and, of course, assuming that our product or service is pleasant and easy to take, it is always best to choose to demonstrate. Naturally, no matter what we are selling, each of us strives to relate the offering to the prospect; to make it so much a part of his life that he can "see" himself enjoying its benefits, and never even dream of being without it. And what better way to accomplish this than to have the product perform?

To expect a catalog page or specification sheet to do the selling job is a sign of sloppy and lazy salesmanship. There is simply no phrase descriptive enough to tell a businessman about the labor-saving features of a machine better than seeing it in action. Is there a word, written or spoken, in your vocabulary that can describe good musical sound to a listener more eloquently than his own ears? And how, besides actually showing her a sample of the results, can you ever truly convey to a housewife just how genuinely white her clothes can be?

Some students of human nature claim that demonstrations accomplish much more than simply substituting for descriptive phrases. "Getting the customer into the act," they say, is an important form of social intercourse. There are ample grounds to suspect that this is true. We do know that gentle handling and even stroking is a pleasant sensation and source of comfort associated with our infant days. As we grow older, and relate to individuals other than our parents, it is necessary for us to find more socially acceptable forms of stroking. This gives rise to such expressions as "ego massaging," but the hunger for the type of recognition that only physical contact can give never leaves us, nor do we ever seem to have enough of it. With both the salesman and prospect turning knobs, flicking switches, or touching a fabric, albeit at different times, these analysts claim, the product serves as a contact go-between, providing the same pleasurable sensations that we subconsciously recall from childhood.

Whether or not one subscribes to such psychological reasoning, there is no doubt that a good demonstration can be a most effective sales tool. If we remember that the prospect is hardly ever interested in acquiring the item for its own sake, but rather for what it can *do* for him, this should not be too difficult to appreciate. Furthermore, we must never succumb to falling in love with our own words, so that our loyalties are divided between what we say and the subject of our remarks. Unfortunately, our sales floors are already too full of salespeople who just can't seem to stop talking. The main objective, let us never forget, is to wed the prospect to the product, and attempting this without a demonstration is much the same as marrying a man to a woman he has never met.

If the goal is better to enable the potential customer to "picture himself" using the item, it should be apparent that we are once more confronted with an exercise in imagination that we already know marks the more successful salesman. This time, though, it is the salesman who must serve as the catalyst, and the prospect whose imagination must be stimulated. The methodology, however, is not unlike that for improving your own capacity which you learned in Chapter 1.

For the most rewarding demonstration, you will want your prospect to be as comfortable as possible. Ideally, he will be both physically and emotionally at ease. This is surely good advice for any sales situation, but it is doubly important when we are attempting to get a prospective customer totally involved. Watch for those small but significant clues that tell you exactly how he is feeling at the moment. If he's walking around with long ashes on his cigarette, he may be more concerned with finding an ashtray than in taking part in your little product drama. Likewise, if the weather is either extremely hot or cold, there is a good chance that he will be more interested in his creature comforts than in anything you can show him at that time. And don't overlook those emotional distractions. We can hardly expect a mother with a crying child to give us her undivided attention, or a businessman hurrying to a luncheon appointment with a customer of his own to play the role we've assigned him in our demonstration.

The technical description for what we're seeking is a "concentration of awareness." In our case, this means channeling the prospect's attention to what we're selling and at the same time excluding as many distracting influences as possible. This is one reason why it is a good idea to have a separate room off the sales floor set aside for this purpose; or, if we are arranging a home demonstration, to select a time when we can reasonably expect the transaction to proceed uninterrupted. If we must demonstrate on a crowded sales floor, we can at least make certain that we will not be called away to answer phone calls, serve other customers, or do anything to interfere with the atmosphere of concentration we are attempting to achieve.

A word or two is in order, here, about the actual setting for our demonstration. More than just a relatively secluded spot is necessary. The best place, as any door-to-door salesman knows, is right in the customer's home or office. Equally essential is the exact spot on those premises. Despite the fact that most salesmen would never think of demonstrating a food blender in the living room, many of them would never hesitate to place their demonstrator machine atop the purchasing agent's desk. Of course, he'll answer no if you ask: "Do you mind if I place this here?" but he will approach your product with a more receptive frame of mind if you think to use the secretary's desk, or wherever the machine will be permanently installed, for demonstration purposes.

In this same area, the problems of a salesman in a retail store demonstrating a product for home use are somewhat more difficult. A separate demonstration room may give one the privacy he needs to capture the prospect's attention; but, unless it is furnished in a homelike setting, it still won't be much help in assisting the customer to visualize the item in everyday use. Lamps, paintings, and other decorations surrounding the central product, but occupying little if any valuable sales floor space, are the answers here. Naturally, the exact type of display that will do the best selling job will depend upon the customer's taste, but that's why good sales floors have more than one demonstration model.

Holding a prospect's attention and moving it along toward a sale is very much the same as landing a big fish. You have to make certain that, in your enthusiasm and desire to reach a close quickly, you don't pull too hard on the line. Give him time to think about what he is seeing and what you are saying. At this stage of a demonstration it will be helpful, too, to recall the use to which the product will be put, and commence your "show" there. In other words, start with the end result. An office manager in the market for a photocopy machine will be far more interested in the quality of the reproduction than in a description of the process by which it is made. He will be more apt to take a letter in his hand than any chemical-laden roller or even a piece of negative paper. These things surely have a bearing on the eventual sale, but for this moment we want to put our best sales foot forward, and that means demonstrating what the product will do.

"This letter was speedily and inexpensively reproduced on the machine I'm demonstrating today," the salesman may say. If he is selling a consumer product such as a television receiver, he can just as easily point to the crystal-clear picture on the screen and remark: "Your entire family can enjoy that quality television viewing in your home tonight." This is what the sales experts mean when they refer to "selling the sizzle instead of the steak," and it cannot be repeated often enough.

Your next step, to be taken as rapidly as possible after the last, is to get the prospect to work the equipment. Notice that the aim is to have the *customer* manipulate the controls, twirl the dial, or what have you. Certainly you can do it better—at least, with your expert's knowledge we must assume that you are more skillful than an individual who may be seeing the product for the first time—but, unless your professional services are part of the transaction, don't show off! Instead, patiently direct the potential customer to the correct knob or switch. Permit him to observe that he already possesses the skill necessary for getting the results he is after.

At this point, it is essential that you make a value judgment. In the vast majority of instances, you will find it advisable to demonstrate the simplicity of operation of whatever it is you are selling. (There are other places the prospect can go if he is seeking an engineering degree.) This is particularly true if you are selling a piece of machinery to a woman or a cooking utensil to a man. And this is also why you will want to keep your directions short and clear.

On the other hand, there will be times when it will be more ego-satisfying to the prospect for you to actually build a little difficulty into using the product. We are reminded, here, of the experience of a cake-mix manufacturer who succeeded in perfecting a mix that required nothing but the addition of a little water to turn out a perfect cake. The only trouble with the product was that it just did not sell. Searching for a reason for this failure, a marketing team discovered that the housewife prospects felt a trifle guilty using the sure-fire mix. It was, after all, stripping them of some of their expertise. When the manufacturer changed his formula so that it was necessary to add an egg or two in addition to the water, sales really soared.

Assuming, though, that yours is the more typical presentation, in which simplicity of operation is a product benefit, do not hide the fact by doing it yourself. If the prospect does make a mistake in using the item, turn this to advantage by accenting the rugged construction of the product, and the speed with which an error can be corrected. Don't be afraid. Everyone wants to get into the act, to try things for themselves, especially before they buy them. They expect to be a little clumsy at first, and may even apologize for it, but the salesman who shrugs this off with a "I made the same mistake myself until I discovered that this small button here gives me perfect results" has a better chance of making the sale.

Throughout the demonstration, it is a good idea to speak of "your" machine. This will aid the customer in imagining that he has already purchased it. Give him a further boost by using as many of his "props" as possible in your drama. For instance, if you are selling a record- or tape-playing instrument, skillful questioning in the "qualifying" stage of the sale will reveal his taste in music. Then, during the demonstration phase, make certain that this is the type of recording used. Returning to our photocopier prospect, the reader can readily appreciate the value of reproducing a letter from the customer's files instead of one put out by sales headquarters for demonstration purposes. And, surely, none of us would buy a chair simply because the salesman looked so comfortable sitting in it. We would, rightfully, wish to try it ourselves.

The subject of "free" home or office trials is one on which the sales community as a whole is fairly evenly divided. There are those who view this method of selling as a natural extension to this business of making it easier for the customer to visualize ownership of the product. They are so positive that what they are selling will "fill the bill" that they unhesitatingly permit the prospect to sample its use, at his convenience, for a specified period. They bank upon the product remaining sold because, among other reasons, the user will not want to bother returning it, or will not wish to suffer a prestige loss by having family or friends imagine that he cannot afford to pay for it.

Opponents of the home-trial method of demonstrating a product's effectiveness admit these advantages, but see more disadvantages. Aside from falling prey to the unscrupulous customer (there are those, too, you know) who will use the trial period to get a particular job accomplished and then return the product, they fear discovering one day that too much of their firm's working capital is invested in demonstration units. They are concerned, also, with the necessity for finding a "used" market for those items which do not stay sold. Finally, they recognize the fact that placing a prospect under even a moral obligation to buy is not the correct method to build a list of satisfied customers. Most of us imagine that we already carry too many obligations. In the flush of excitement over a new product we may add just one more, but when the honeymoon is over this is the first we will try to avoid.

Home demonstrations or not, though, there is no better way to sell anything than to put it in the prospect's hands. Far from shirking his sales responsibilities, the salesman who uses this technique has his work cut out for him in guiding the demonstration to a successful conclusion. He is responsible for staging the sale in just the right atmosphere. He must be able, on very short notice, to teach his customers how to operate the product, be artful in directing the "play" to the end use, and skillful in pointing out extra benefits, such as weight or rugged construction, without distracting his prospect's attention. The result of all this, as we shall discover in Chapter 11, is an easier sales "close" and a more prosperous salesman.

Chapter 9

Trading Up

Despite the fact that over 60 percent of the sales in all the product lines in the United States are confined to an average of just two models in any one line, the typical salesman today carries many more than that number in his model mix. There are low-priced units to appeal to the price-conscious shopper and deluxe pieces for the status-seeker, with innumerable variations in between. Indeed, it almost appears as if industry's answer to any situation in which supply overtakes demand is to produce still more models in the hope that everyone will find something in the expanded line to meet his requirements.

Although this state of affairs may denote a field day for the customer, there is no denying that it places a burden on the salesman that the pioneers in this business never experienced. Today we have to be more knowledgeable about more model features, be familiar with more prices, and, most important, be in a better position to explain the differences to customers than ever before. Even if we do not go door to door selling our merchandise, the figurative weight of so many variations on the same product tends to be overpowering. Surely we owe ourselves, if not the customer, some further explanation of this phenomenon and, if possible, an insight into how we might turn the development to profitable advantage.

In the retailing field, at least, the surfeit of models on the sales floor is principally due to the necessity to cover a number of "price points," or prices at which different groups of customers can be expected to be attracted to the store. Oh, yes, the uses to which a product may be put will vary from one customer to the next, but if this was the honest-to-goodness reason for model variations we could settle for the one that has all the features—to be used as the customer wills—and save ourselves a great deal of trouble. No, much as we may despise the shopper who "knows the price of everything and the value of nothing," for example, there is no doubt that price alone is important to a large segment of the buying public. This is particularly true in these days of better-educated consumers, with their endless sources for obtaining product details, and the emphasis on national "brand-name" selling, in which some of the most vital retailing functions have been assumed by the manufacturer or wholesaler. In the latter instance, the theory is that the consumer will be somewhat presold on the product as a result of national promotions. The local salesman, therefore, will have an easier job making the "close."

Be that as it may, this marketing concept leaves the retailer who relies upon advertising for a majority of his prospects with just two choices. He can either promote his "branded" wares at competitive prices, which often means negative profit, or he can omit price entirely from his ads, trusting that his salesmen will have an opportunity to tell the "value" story to potential customers. Unfortunately, the public has been so indoctrinated to seeing price in ads that the merchant who elects to go the latter route sees only a selected clientele of people who have purchased from him before. Furthermore, it should be apparent that, to be really effective in the former instance, it is practically necessary to meet or be close to the lowest price in the community.

These "promotional leaders," as they are called, are, quite obviously, less functional models with which the customer, once he learns the facts, is seldom satisfied. However, they do accomplish the task of drawing "traffic" to the store. Because of this, outside of sales circles they are frequently referred to as "bait" models, the implication being that there is something morally dishonest about their promotion since the intention of the store is to sell the customer something quite different and more expensive. Nothing could be more slanderous to the selling profession.

There are dishonest merchants, of course, but the vast majority know that their bread is buttered on the side of satisfied customers. If they advertise a product, no matter how unprofitably priced it may be, they are fully prepared to sell and deliver it. Instead of wasting their time attempting to circumvent federal laws against misleading advertising, they devote their energies to sharpening their skills in telling the customer why he needs something other than the promotional leader *that attracted him to the store.* That is the only reason for the existence of these models. They serve to satisfy the public's unquenchable thirst for a "bargain," and are the starting point for the game of "trading goods" that eventually leads to a sale.

By now, the reader should know precisely how this game is played. Usually the customer makes the first move by offering the advertised price for a product. When he realizes how little real good (benefit) he will receive in return for his money, he draws back, hesitatingly, while the salesman throws more benefits into his side of the sales scale. At a certain, predetermined point the salesman pauses, because the trade is in balance. He has gone as far as he can in meeting the prospect's offer. If the potential customer wants more good for his money he must load the scale once more, prompting the salesman to step to a "better" model. And so it goes, this game of trading goods, back and forth. Occasionally it is the customer who assumes the initiative, but more often it is the salesman who sweetens the pot by talking about and demonstrating what else is available. Because profits are generally keyed to price, the seller can be expected to strive to sell the "top of the line," and his success is measured in terms of how far up the model ladder he goes. This method of play is known as "trading up," a procedure that begins with an advertised leader, and which, if played to a conclusion, cannot fail to result in happier salesmen *and customers.*

Although it is difficult to generalize, the next step above the "promotional leader" in most lines is the "low-end comparison" model. To be most effective, this higher-priced unit must have easily demonstrable features that are truly different and better than those found on the leader. There are moments in the sale when talk of such features as chrome trim and colorful lights are in order, but this is not one of them. "For just a few dollars more," the salesman should honestly be able to say, "you can own this one, which is so much better suited to your needs." In practice, it is advisable to place this unit some distance from the promotional-priced one. Also, as we shall presently discover, it is a good idea *not* to use this one for purposes of demonstration.

Moving to this model does give the salesman another chance to qualify his prospect. If he is genuinely interested in a product that will perform well, the customer will not resist the move. This is the time, too, to verify our opinion of what the prospect can afford to pay. Perhaps our advertised price is really as high as he can go. If so, it is infinitely better to discover it now while we still have an opportunity to graciously retreat to the leader. Far too many salesmen, however, take this backward step at the first sign of resistance. Naturally our prospect will tend to balk at paying more than he has offered—until we give him a good reason why he should do just that. The delicate operation involves giving strict attention to the price the customer says he can meet, but leading him with a feature or two found on the low-end comparison piece. The salesman who settles for a sale at this level, though, is really doing only half his job.

Every experienced sales organization has what we call a "sell" model. This one, priced higher than the low-end comparison unit, is the item we truly desire to "move." It meets all the requirements of our company insofar as profits are concerned, but it obviously must do more than that. All too often the "sell" piece is determined exclusively by the accounting department. Actually, it should represent the combined thinking of all the business managers, particularly the sales head. Through contact with customers, he, more than the others, knows the features that satisfy a majority of his prospects, and he is probably well aware of the value of each of these.

Successful salesmen are always completely informed about the "sell" model. More important than the model number are the reasons why it has been selected for this exalted position in the line. Someone must have thought it was admirably suited for the spot, and that "someone" most likely was the boss. Rather than question the decision, therefore, the salesman who is slated for better things in the organization will make every effort to understand it. On what basis is the higher price justified? What are the distinguishing features of this specific product? How can its extra features be translated into consumer benefits? (We shall have more to say about that one shortly.) What is the best method to communicate the value of the "sell" model above all others, and, value for value, how does the price of this unit compare with competition? Armed with the answers to those questions, the salesman should have little difficulty in stepping once more—this time from the "low-end comparison" to the "sell" unit.

Because this transition is the most crucial of all, it would be rewarding to concentrate on more specific methods for making the move. For one thing, we can make a distinction between two words—*features* and *benefits*—which we have been using somewhat interchangeably, but which have differences vital to the successful conclusion of a sale. Knowledge of these differences is another factor that separates the professionals from the amateurs in this business. It is so essential, in fact, that the salesman who really wants to get ahead in his work will run, not walk, to prepare lists of each for all the models he is selling now.

Features are all of the additions or changes in the product that make it perform better than the original use for which it was developed. They are easily recognized components of whatever it is we are selling, and that influence its use and/or appearance. It is possible, for example, to receive radio signals on a wet-cell-powered, crystal-detector receiver. The reception of wireless transmissions was exactly what Marconi had in mind when he invented the radio. On the other hand, few of us would dream of buying a receiver today without a loudspeaker to replace the origi-

nal earphones, a convenient tuning control instead of the
old "cat's whisker," and a more satisfactory source of
power, such as a line cord to house current or dry cells
for our portable set. All of these features have been developed since the first radio was marketed, and there is every
reason to believe that we are far from finished improving
this product's appeal to the public, despite the fact that
there are some 150 million radios in use today.

In many instances, features are of just such a mechanical
or technical nature, but they can encompass change in style
as well. The apparel and automobile industries with their
annual model changes offer good examples of how design
can be a feature leading, indirectly, to a sale. The main
thing to remember is that a feature is something to which
a salesman can point, and around which he can create a
portion of his sales pitch. But, although there are some
people to whom being "first on the block" with a feature,
no matter how useless it may be, is all important, the
salesman who expects his prospects to become enthused
automatically over a change in the product is making a
grave mistake. It is imperative that he learn how to trans-
late these features into *benefits*.

In the case of the radio features noted above, these
benefits are obvious. Loudspeakers eliminate the need for
heavy, cumbersome headphones. The tuning control enables us to locate stations quickly and effortlessly. And the
newer power sources make it possible for the radio listener
to enjoy home entertainment without the bother of re-
charging batteries, while those tiny receivers with their dry
cells give us all the benefits of true portability. It can be
readily observed, with this example before us, that benefits
are no more than interpretations of features as they apply
to the customer. That is exactly why, of the two, benefits

are more important. (The salesman is interested in all of his product's features, but the customer is more selective in the benefits about which he wishes to hear.) Of course, as we have repeatedly demonstrated, the advantages of any product change can be psychological, physical, or both. Running boards on old cars are still considered to be most practical by some people. Yet the most popular notion that the unbroken lines of modern automobiles are more "stylish" made the design change eliminating running boards a benefit just as surely as if the industry had perfected an engine that could operate with no other fuel than water. Naturally, it would be difficult to assign an equal value to these two changes, but each is a benefit just the same.

Preparing a list of features and benefits for the product you are selling can be a good exercise in customer empathy. (This would be as applicable to the individual who was trying to "sell" himself to a prospective employer. The applicant's honesty is one of his good features, leading to the benefit that he can be trusted.) Commence with the features. List them all, no matter how slight, bearing in mind that someone considered them of sufficient value to incorporate into the item. Then, next to each of these write the benefit or benefits a sales prospect can be expected to derive from the feature. In addition to discovering more pegs on which you can hang your sales message, you may find one or two features so technical in nature that you will want to avoid them when speaking with most prospects. Never forget that, even with the plethora of models available today there are still some features that have no benefit to a certain class of customers.

Returning to our model display, we find that we have at least three basic units in the line—a promotional leader, a low-end comparison piece, and the sell model. The well-rounded line, however, will have a minimum of one additional number. This, for want of a better term, we shall call the "high-end comparison" piece.

Actually, firms that offer a high-end comparison model have little intention of selling it. The product is available, of course, for customers who will settle for nothing but the "finest," and this one has everything. Here is where the fancy trim, construction that will outlast the product's useful life, and all the gadgets are displayed. Most of these features, which add considerably to the price, making this the most expensive model in the line, are not essential to the smooth performance of the product. They do, however, fill a very practical need for the salesman, by enabling him to demonstrate that he is not primarily interested in selling the most expensive number in the store. To put not only this but the entire basic four-piece line in its proper perspective, let us follow a typical sale to its happy conclusion.

"Good morning, madam. How may we serve you?" a salesman may greet his first prospect of the day.

"I'd like to see the model you advertised in last night's newspaper."

"Certainly. It's right over here. When it was produced, it was considered to be the finest, most reliable piece of its kind. Since then, of course, the engineers have learned much more about what customers such as you really want in this type of product. For example, over here we have one of the latest models, incorporating practically all of the improvements any wise shopper might wish."

Observe how effortlessly the salesman has moved his customer to the low-end comparison unit. If he encounters little resistance, he steps to the third model and says:

"Personally, for just a few extra dollars, I would rather have this one. In fact, this is the same model as the one

I own. It has every important engineering change you could want, and it has given us excellent, trouble-free service."

Hopefully, the salesman has now made his sale. There exists the possibility, though, that the prospect will balk at the price, which is now more than she intended to pay— before she heard the feature-benefit story. In that case, the salesman guides her to the high-end comparison unit.

"This is absolutely the finest number in the line," he states. "Notice how it sparkles. Of course, despite the fact that it's priced much higher than the one we were just considering, it doesn't do anything more. It just looks nicer. You would be paying for those extra frills. Back over here, you can save money and get all the benefits of owning the most expensive version."

All of which brings us to the subjects of meeting customer objections and "closing" the sale. We shall see how simply these obstacles, too, can be overcome.

Chapter 10

Overcoming Objections— or Every Knock Is a Boost

A salesman's life would be oh so sweet, if all transactions went according to the book—if prospects would ask just the right questions and be content with one of the carefully-rehearsed answers, if the product line was really broad enough to satisfy the wants of every potential buyer, and if nobody ever disputed the claims we make for what we're selling. Unfortunately, in the very real world of face-to-face selling, these "dream" situations seldom exist. Or is it so unfortunate?

When we pause to think about it, practically and philosophically, we are not so positive that we would wish for too many of those "easy" sales. In the first place, as we have repeatedly stated, questions and objections are really opportunities, thinly disguised, for the salesman to further qualify his customer and to justify his existence on the marketing scene. Without these interruptions, selling would be something we could leave to order-takers or vending machines, because there would be no need for personalized answers or for someone to relate the product to an individual need. In fact, the extreme version of such a way of life might be a society in which people would be as machines to be "programmed" by some super-being (call him an "advertising genius," if you will) to follow his dictates—our second fear. They would, in the literal sense of the word, be slaves, unable to think, no matter how imperfectly, for themselves. And, instead of teaching others his secret, the one individual with all that power would either use it for his selfish ends, or innocently lead his sheeplike followers down wrong pathways because there would be no one to question his judgment.

We are pleased to confess, therefore, that no suggestion in this book will work 100 percent of the time. It is also apparent that the reader does not have a foolproof selling technique of his own. If he did, he would not spend time looking for a hint of a better method here. When we put these two observations together, it is clear that no piece of writing or talk on the subject can be complete without somehow accounting for our errors and omissions. That is also what those questions and objections represent. A question implies that we have failed adequately to cover a point in which the prospect is interested—an error in judgment on our part. An objection, on the other hand, is another way of the prospect saying, "You have failed to sell me"—the omission of a clinching argument. The real pros in this business, as we shall soon learn, may deliberately leave the opportunity for questions and objections in their sales presentations, but, whether or not they are done on purpose, they are errors.

Mistakes in selling, it is safe to say, come to light faster than most others we make in our daily lives. We detect them, first and foremost, in the failure of the prospect to buy—a subject that will be more thoroughly covered in the next chapter. They may be seen, too, in the type of questions the customer raises during the sale. "Will this fit into the corner of the living room I want to decorate?" or, "Can I use this machine without hiring additional help?" are just other ways of saying, "I am not convinced that this will fit the space," or, "I'm afraid this will be too costly a machine to operate." Such *questions,* the reader will probably recognize, are merely *objections* in another form, and so the two words will be used interchangeably in the balance of this chapter.

Many a perfectionist sales authority believes that the best way to overcome objections is to avoid them, to make certain that they never happen. Well, we imagine that we covered that bit of fantasy earlier, but there is something to be said for avoiding certain objections. The customer who complains about price, for one, probably was not originally correctly qualified. Can he or can he not afford to pay the price? That is the question the answer to which the salesman should have before he is too long into the sale. A second question—does he or does he not consider the item worth the price?—is one the salesman is trying to answer all during the sale. That's the name of the game. Remember? When the answer to that second one is yes, the sale is made.

On the whole, though, the best we can do with objections is to learn to meet them. Then we can profit by the mistake, and build the answer into subsequent sales talks, so that other prospects will not bring us the same objection. This is one of the two best arguments for listening carefully to every question the prospect asks, and even jotting it down as quickly as possible so that we will not forget to prepare the answer before we greet the next customer. The second reason, obviously, is that we cannot make the sale by responding to questions we do not hear; that would be too costly a lesson.

The type of objections you are most apt to hear can result from five different sets of circumstances. First, the prospect simply was not listening when you covered the very point to which he is objecting. Second, he is unfamiliar with the product, and, rather than admit his ignorance, expresses it in the form of an objection. Third, he just does not believe you. Fourth, he cannot afford the price, but will not say so. And, fifth, he never seriously intended to buy, and was shopping for either information or companionship.

It is to our advantage to explore each of these types of objections in depth—they can tell us much about our sales techniques and the prospect before us, and each requires just a little different type of handling. However, there is one rule that can be expressed in one word—*concede*—and that can be profitably applied to all objections. Prospects are no different from salesmen in that they all have their share of vanity, and no one of them likes to hear that he is wrong. That's why the "yes, but" method, or agreeing with the objection while you are preparing to counter it, can work wonders with all prospects. Of course, we must often be more sophisticated in our methods of conceding. Never underestimating the intelligence of your customer is another good habit to cultivate, but with a little bit of practice you can develop refinements of your own. For a starter, you might mull over some of these:

"I wondered the same thing myself, until . . ." or,

"That very problem bothered us right here in the store, until . . ." or,

"I'm so glad you raised that point," or,

"That is an excellent question," or,

"My last customer mentioned the same thing. I told him
. . ." or,

"Most people would not have noticed that, but . . ." or,

"That's the very question this product is designed to
answer."

You can probably come up with many more. The main
point to remember is that commissions or salaries are never
tied to winning arguments, but to making sales. Also, there
are no trivial questions, just disinterested salesmen. If the
prospect thinks it is important enough to ask, it is vital that
you see it the same way. So hold your temper, bite the
bullet or what have you, but get in there and sell the way
the prospect wants you to.

The customer who isn't listening can be most aggravat-
ing. This situation may necessitate your going over the
same ground several times, and none of us is so egotistical
that he can stand the sound of his voice saying the same
things for very long. Yet much of this can be avoided if
you will try to capture the nonlistener's attention with a
question or two of your own. Don't forget, though, to avoid
mechanical yes or no answers by keeping your questions
open-ended. "Yes, the color selection is smaller this year,
because we are concentrating on just the most fashionable
colors. Do you prefer the green or blue?" will keep the
prospect on his toes, and give you more qualifying information besides.

Here, too, you can try opening the door for a question
by deliberately saying something to stimulate the customer.
If he is in the market for a piece of electrical equipment,
you might make the statement that yours will operate on
any 220-volt circuit. If that fails to bring the rejoinder:
"You mean it won't work on 115 volts?" you haven't lost

much, because you can always follow it up with a question of your own about the voltage available. In either case, you are doing something to capture the prospect's attention.

Closely allied to the person who raises objections indicating that he has not been listening is the individual who doesn't say anything. Surely, you've run across this bird. He just stands there with a faraway look in his eyes, and objects by not agreeing. We shall meet this prospect again at closing time. During the sale, however, he can be most discouraging, if you let him. Next time you meet him, though, try going back to the lessons you learned about qualifying. More often than not you'll discover that you failed to pinpoint this customer's needs. Go all the way back to his wants, if necessary, but get him talking about himself and his desires. "Did you say that you were looking for something three or four feet wide?" you might inquire, even if you already know the answer. Then, take it from there and see how fast those silent objections are overcome.

Getting the prospect to listen, or holding his attention, even when he comes to the salesman obviously seeking something, is more than half the job in selling. That is exactly why questions from customers who are apparently not listening should be encouraged. They are a sign that we have sparked some interest, or that we are wasting our time on a model which does not meet his requirements. In either case, the questions should be viewed as allies, and must never be answered with a "I told you that five minutes ago." If the prospect did not hear the answer, it is the same as if you never said it, and we must be thankful that he has given us the opportunity to repeat ourselves.

Of all the objectors, the one who is unfamiliar with the product but who doesn't want us to know it is the most common. You can recognize this prospect by his raising questions that you considered to be too trivial to answer beforehand, or ones that may have been covered in an extensive national advertising campaign for the past few years. But before you even think, "Where has this joker been all this while?" stop and consider. Someone has invested in your training, and you have chosen to make a career out of whatever it is you are selling. These factors, combined, have given you an expert's outlook on the product. As we have stated, be thankful that the customer lacks the expertise of a salesman, and show him more than a small amount of patience.

You may know that your entire industry has been producing products that operate on alternating current for the past decade or more, but the prospect who questions if the item will perform satisfactorily on his AC outlet is to be treated with the same respect as if he announced that he was using atomic power. Engineers are not alone in their fondness for radios, you know.

In matters of fashion or style, this same class of customers, if they are not too conscious of trends, can be led into a mode of living without being aware of it. There simply may not have been anything else they could buy. But suddenly, right there on your sales floor, they realize that the products offered "look different" from the one they purchased ten or more years ago. If they wonder aloud whether the one you want them to buy will fit in with their present furnishings, your task may be to complete the job of customer style education that other salesmen left unfinished. After all, even the most unfashionable of us must have home furnishings and clothes.

In more instances than one might suppose, the prospect will not volunteer the information that he is so lacking in technical knowledge or fashion awareness that he is completely at the salesman's mercy in deciding the best item to buy. He is going to play his cards close to his vest, lest someone take advantage of his ignorance. And finally, to complete his disguise, he will find as many objections as possible to the sale so that the salesman will be compelled to tell him all there is to know about the product. In other words, he is attempting to trick the salesman into doing what the salesman should have been doing all along!

Although we all encounter them—and probably always will—questions from prospects who are obviously unfamiliar with the product are a sign that we have failed to adequately get our message across. They are a reminder that this or that base is still uncovered. Rather than fearing them, therefore, we should encourage objections of this sort. This can be done by inviting the customer to play a bigger role in the sale. The frank statement: "I've spent so much time living with the features of this terrific product that I may overlook something of special interest to you. If I do, please don't hesitate to remind me," can go a long way toward putting a customer at ease. He will be delighted to receive confirmation of the fact that you, too, are human.

One of the best ways to handle objections of the type we have been discussing is to show the prospect that you do take them seriously. You can accomplish this merely by repeating the objection or question. However, to avoid even a hint of mockery when you restate a question for the purpose of answering it, be certain that you use your own words. An echo chamber is a very poor atmosphere in which to buy anything. "I see that you are concerned over whether this machine will operate without any additional wiring," you might say to the customer who is still living in the DC age. "I'm so glad that you asked that question, because this product is guaranteed to perform on your present current." And, to the prospect who has just awakened to the importance of style, you can say: "I, too, would wonder about this fitting in with my present furnishings. Let's see, what type of furniture do you have?"

Any question can be used to advantage by a salesman who listens, and who is thoroughly familiar with his product. If it cannot be converted into a benefit, it can be another step in qualifying the prospect. All that it requires is some practice in listening not for what the customer says but for what he means. Is the objection to size masking a lack of knowledge about the space he has available for it? Is color blindness behind his dislike for the color? Is fear of repair bills the basis for his objection to extra features? (We will presently go into greater depth concerning the fear of price motive.) Remaining alert to the answers to such questions can help the salesman *and customer* over many sales hurdles. At the same time, in using this method to overcome objections there are two major pitfalls, of which we must be aware.

First, there is the danger of being too sensitive to the real reasons behind the prospect's comments. We are reminded, here, of the classic story about two psychoanalysts who meet on the street. "How are you?" the first inquires. "I wonder what he means by that?" the second thinks. By all means, we want to avoid that trap. It is possible to read too much into an objection. Perhaps the customer who inquires about price during the sale of a well-advertised product truly wants to know. He may consider it quite reasonable, but if we take his question as a sign that it is too high, and waste precious minutes justifying it, we may instill doubts where none existed before.

Other questions may be stalls, or attempts to gain more time, because the prospect can't think of anything else to say while he weighs the purchase against some other yardstick. Because we are not skilled analysts, we cannot be expected to unearth those hidden messages. Yet repeating the question and listening for the answer should bring those true meanings closer to the surface of the conversation.

Second, there is the distinct possibility that we may get "hung up" on some objection. This means becoming so preoccupied with the objection that we lose sight of the sale. While we invite questions from customers, and can learn much from them, they are, nevertheless, interruptions in what hopefully is a carefully prepared sales presentation. Unless the objection opens up an entirely new approach to the sale, therefore, it is best to answer it, and get back on the road you have mapped out. Many salesmen, contemplating their lost sales, complain that they are always on the defensive, always reacting to what the customer says rather than leading the conversation. This is due as much as anything else to the salesman being overly interested in winning the argument. We may not realize it, but many of us suffer from this habit. Too late we learn that, even though he may lose this round, the customer, sensing that he has drawn blood in the seller's overreaction, is preparing still another blow. And so we go from one defensive posture to the next, leaving little time for the other, more positive things we can tell the prospect.

Closely related to this problem is the one involving the salesman who is so obsessed with the notion of meeting objections that he thinks this is his entire job. He is, usually, a master of answering questions. In fact he is so good at it, and knows it, that he waits for the next one instead

of going ahead with his business. Generally he does not
have long to wait, but he seldom if ever hears: "Should
I carry it home or have it delivered?" Selling is a positive
act! That is to say, the one who makes the sale has a
well-thought-out program for action that is not based upon
questions. He does not merely say, "This is my product.
Go ahead and ask me about it." He assumes a certain lack
of knowledge on the part of his prospect, remembering
always that it is impossible to anticipate everything the
customer does not know, and builds his campaign around
imparting his expertise.

The most difficult of all the objections to overcome are
those which result from a lack of confidence in the salesman on the part of the prospect. Unless these objections
are handled properly, they make it virtually impossible to
close a sale, but they are usually so well hidden that it takes
a genuine expert to uncover them. In most instances they
result from a poor experience the customer may have had
with either the company or the product, but objections in
this category arising from a personality conflict between
salesman and customer are not unknown. One would suspect that, if such were the case, the prospect would automatically qualify himself, or disqualify himself by not
patronizing the firm, but this is not always so.

People do buy from companies they do not particularly
like, for many reasons. The immediate need may be so
great that they overlook past injustices; or, in their enthusiasm for the item, they rationalize away the reasons for
not buying from a certain salesman. Yet, no matter how
far back in their minds they push these concerns, they are
still there, and they come to the surface in the strangest
ways.

Again, as in the case of the salesman, customers suffer

from the same "instinctive" likes and dislikes as the rest of us. However, being human, they will go out of their way to avoid a direct confrontation. Time is too short, and they may lose. If they are so prejudiced against fat or thin individuals, for example, they will simply avoid contact with these people. And, if they should encounter one on a sales floor, they will certainly not admit to such a prejudice. Instead, they will think, "If I do have to buy from this fellow, I will at least make it as difficult as possible for him." It sounds unreasonable, we admit, but why should we expect members of the unreasonable human race to act rationally just because they are buying? From this type of prospect we can expect to hear such things as: "I was really looking for something else," or, "Is this the only selection you have?"

After several responses such as those, the wise salesman will recognize and appreciate what he is up against. Although the sale is not necessarily lost, it may be more prudent to turn this customer over to another salesman—he will, surely, have the opportunity to do the same for you—with a polite explanation. "Mr. Jones is better acquainted than I with the stock. I am certain that he can assist you." Much as we all hate to admit defeat, in this case discretion may be the better part of valor.

Of course, conditions such as this must not be confused with those in which the customer may have some legitimate reason for lacking confidence in what you are saying. Would you, for instance, take an unqualified "this product will last a lifetime" at its face value? Naturally you would not. Well, neither would your prospect. If, in fact, the life expectancy of your item is one of its sales features, it is best to make this point in terms your customer will find more believable. "Over 80 percent of the models we sold

twenty years ago are still in use," or, "We subject all
of our products to a test the equivalent of ten years' use
in your home," make the point very nicely.

If after all of this you do encounter a "doubting
Thomas," shift to a convincing demonstration. Hit the
product with a hammer, set fire to it, or *do* something to
drive home your point. The significance of this move is
that you will be permitting actions to speak louder than
your unconvincing words. Just make certain that your
"test" conditions are at least as difficult as the customer
can expect to find in his home, office, or factory. If you
do not, you will be paving the way for still more objections.

Another way of establishing your veracity is to invite
the prospect to contact one of your other satisfied customers. Hopefully, in the qualifying stages of the sale, you have
determined which of your users is nearest to the prospect.
Now, with the old customer's permission, of course, you
can invite the prospect to check for himself. This is part
of the "use the user" technique, which can work very well
provided you have first determined that the user is *completely* satisfied.

The prospect who has previously had a disagreeable
experience with the firm is even easier to handle. He has,
after all, taken the first step toward letting bygones be
bygones by coming back. It would be foolhardy, therefore,
to do less than meet him halfway. Don't bring up the past!
If it is still on his mind, he will do it without too much
prompting. (You have already prepared yourself for this
eventuality by inquiring if he has purchased from you
before.) Once you detect that the old wound has not completely healed, you can forestall any mention of it by
casually speaking of all the steps you have taken since he
last purchased to eliminate the possibility of the problem
recurring. He may want to get a last ounce of satisfaction

by raising new objections based on the old. However, armed with the "yes, but" technique, you can meet these easily.

Although they are far from the most difficult to overcome, objections based on price are far more numerous in the experience of practically all salesmen. The bald truth is that price is never low enough, no matter how big a value the purchase represents. If everyone gave merchandise away for the asking, customers would soon be looking for someone who made free deliveries. This is all part of the natural, and understandable, reluctance of people to part with money. The more mature individuals may appreciate that they can never expect to receive more value than they are prepared to give, but nearly everyone is on the defensive when it comes to this part of the sale, and the best defense is still a good offense. In this case, this means an objection.

As you might imagine, these objections come in a variety of forms and sizes. An extreme but good example is to be found in a tale from Jewish folklore. It seems that members of the religious community in a small Polish town were attempting to raise funds for a house of worship. High on their list were two of the wealthiest citizens, who had always been most charitable. This time, however, the first of these refused to give. Business had not been too good of late, he obviously lied, and sent the committee that had called on him on its way. When they explained what had happened to the second man, he too refused to contribute. Pressed for a reason, he replied: "I don't like apple pie."

"But what does apple pie have to do with our synagogue?" the startled committee members asked.

"Nothing," the rich man said. "But when you don't want to give, one excuse is as good as another."

Your customers may cover their motives better than that,

but the result is the same. There are those cases, of course, where the prospect will come right out and say that he cannot afford it. Such people, though, are few in number. Instead, they will find every reason to squirm out of the predicament into which you may, inadvertently, have put them—facing up to the fact that their supply of money is limited. The best solution, after first qualifying the prospect to avoid ever getting into this situation, is to give him a graceful "out" so that he doesn't have to search for an "apple pie" solution.

Sensing that the objection may be rooted in the pocketbook, you can say, "We build value into all of our models, but know that everyone can't use all of the features. Would you prefer this with the automatic operation or that with the manual controls?" Notice that the word "price" is deliberately not used here, and that we have given the customer a perfect rationale for his real objection. There is little to be gained from rubbing his nose in the fact that he can't afford to buy the "best," and, rather than send this prospect to a more sympathetic competitor, it is more profitable for us to take him out of the market by selling him the product for which he can pay.

The customer who openly objects to price is not always unable to meet it. Let us not make the mistake of thinking so rigidly. In some instances, the prospect may simply be unconvinced as to the value offered. He is prepared to buy, but only if we can prove to him that he is getting his money's worth, something that we may have failed to do so far. The salesman who encounters and recognizes this state of affairs is lucky. He is getting a second chance at selling his "value" story, assuming that he attempted to do so in the first place. Here, though, the tale becomes more difficult to tell, because no two of us have the same notion of value.

Who is to say how much anything is worth? You can offer a person who is *not* in the market for an automobile the finest car at half its sales price, and not get a glimmer of interest. But selling the prospect who is already in the market is a different story. Value to him is based upon the use to which the machine will be put, and therein lies a clue to meeting this objection.

If your customer complains about price, and the objection is not an excuse to get out of the sale or purchase, you have obviously failed to balance that sales scale. Mentally return to our discussion of separating "wants" from "needs" and reexamine the latter. Do you know what the customer can truly use, or did you stop listening when he related his desires? If you correctly appraise those needs, you can always relate them to price—in terms that the prospect will understand. If you encounter difficulty, maybe you are still back there catering to his wants, and both of you are indulging in a fantasy that is not worth any price.

Our last category of objections are those that come from persons who have absolutely no intention of buying now, no matter what the salesman says. Oh, they won't admit it, of course. Instead, they will seize upon any one of a number of objections. Their stated reasons may range from, "I have to discuss this with my wife (husband, partner, boss, etc.)," to, "I'll be back." In some instances these objections may be valid, and we surely do not want to write all of these off as hopeless. But, if you meet delaying tactics of this sort, and, after countering them, find yourself with yet another objection on your hands, it is safe to assume that you are talking to a "shopper." Such individuals, all too familiar to most salesmen, may be classified into one of three distinct groups.

First, and easiest to dispose of, is the professional shopper. He is a cross that almost all salesmen must bear sometime in their careers. There is not much to be said about this fellow, who can be anything from a competitor to a government agent. Because he is trained in his work, difficult to spot, and easy to confuse with genuine prospects, we must exercise great care that we treat all customers with the same tact and care. Good salesmen have few secrets anyway, so there is nothing to be lost, aside from time, in giving the professional buyer our undivided attention. The faster we get him out of the way, the sooner we can get back to selling customers who really count.

Our second nonbuyer is more to be pitied than censured. He is the person to whom shopping, particularly for things he cannot afford to buy, is an exhilarating experience. Remember? We did say that all people enjoy shopping. Well, to those with nothing better to do with their time, it may be their sole source of enjoyment. These are the lonely, frustrated individuals who are hungry for a personal relationship or just the sound of a human voice. They are the personification of all the lonely, worthless feelings we all have at one time or another. More important, they represent *potential* customers—maybe not today, but at some time in the future. As such, they must be treated with every courtesy that time will allow.

We should never forget the importance of "word of mouth" advertising. A salesman's success, as we now know, depends as much upon what people think of him as it does upon what they think of his product. Assuming, therefore, that we go out of our way to make a good impression on a prospect who doesn't buy, but he relays his feelings to six other people and each of these tells six others, and so on, in just ten short steps our list of prospects will look like this:

1

6

36

216

1296

7776

46,656

279,936

1,679,616

10,077,696

Over 10 million! Surely, that is worth the extra moment or two we might spend with someone who cannot buy now.

The prospect who has no intention of making the purchase because he is shopping for comparative information on which to base a decision later—our third type—is another matter. His very determination to not place the order is another signal that we have failed somewhere along the line. There is no denying that, but his case is far from hopeless. Some salesmen, after trying all else, leave these customers with a "burn" price, or a figure that they know to be far below anything the competition can offer, and that they themselves are not prepared to meet. At least, they think, it will bring the prospect back. This tactic does not make sense. It fails to take into account the fact that most people are interested in value, not price alone, and the ability of the customer (with or without the assistance of a competitor) to see through this trick. It is poetic justice when the customer returns and insists that the item be sold at the low price quoted.

A little imagination applied to the problem of the comparison shopper can turn up more ethical solutions. More than one salesman, realizing that his prospect is moving through the market place, has presented his customer with a quart of ice cream or some other gift that cannot conveniently be carried around. Others have gone the home demonstration route, and still more have actually made comparison shopping easier for their customers by listing pertinent product features (and benefits) they know the competition does not have. Naturally, it is best to close the sale on the spot, but, when every attempt has been tried and failed, it is advisable to "lose" gracefully, and make every effort to contact the prospect later to get in a last word before the decision is made.

Objections of any sort are definitely troublesome. They keep us from our goal, and because they are hardly ever anticipated, they can be unnerving. However, the salesman who does not prepare himself for this eventuality is living in a fool's paradise. Such preparation, though, as we have been attempting to demonstrate, is not difficult. It does require a mustering of intellectual and emotional resources. And these, not unlike the muscles of an athlete, are developed only through constant training. To put yourself in the best shape to meet any refusal of the customer to buy, there is nothing better than a solid dose of product knowledge peppered with just the right amount of humility. This combination, frequently reinforced, should give you the strength to surmount any hurdle the customer may put in your path to a sale.

Chapter 11

Closing the Sale

Quickly now! Which sock, the right or the left, do you put on first each morning? Which side of your face do you shave first?

If you paused to think about the answers, rather than blurting them out, there is nothing wrong with your memory or reflexes. Few people would be able to snap out the answers. We all do certain things, such as dressing and shaving, so frequently, and in exactly the same manner, so regularly, that these acts become habits. As such, they do not require much conscious thought. Indeed, we use this time, while our fingers are busy, thinking about other things, such as how we will greet the first new prospect of the day. Life is so full of new and exciting experiences that we do not choose to waste time thinking about habits.

For many professional salesmen, *closing*, or successfully concluding a sale by getting the order, is not much different from dressing. It is an important part of the day, but one that is done so often in a lifetime that they do not think about how they do it. That is, it never occurs to them until there is a noticeable and otherwise unexplainable drop in their sales. Then it becomes the most crucial happening in the business world, because salesmen are not graded on the way they greet prospects. Nor are they paid on the basis of how many times and how well they demonstrate a product. Whether their compensation is salary or commission, their success is related directly to the number of closes they make. Nothing can change that, and that is why, even at the peak of their careers, the better salesmen are scrutinizing and sharpening their closing skills.

Hopefully, the reader, too, is in this self-improvement-seeking category.

To improve a close, we must first understand exactly what it is. There is so much misinformation about that this may be easier said than done. For one thing, it is far more than taking or even asking for the customer's order. Insofar as the prospect is concerned, by the time we get to the close, he has come full circle in expressing his wants. Originally, you will recall, he came to us with a want. It became our job to separate that want from his needs so that we could concentrate on a product or service we could sell him. Now that we have accomplished our task so far, all that remains is for the prospect, with or without our help, to want whatever it is we are selling.

In theory, that is a close. In practice, there is much more to closing because, even after he reaches that last wanting stage, and unless it is an impulse purchase made on the spur of the moment, the prospect will not volunteer his desires without at least some further prompting from the salesman. That is, after leading his customer with carefully-thought-out questions throughout the sale, the salesman finally puts him in a position where it is much easier to say yes than no to the all-important "Shall I write up the order?" As we will shortly learn, the words will probably be different, but the objective is a successful close.

In other words, a close is one final spoken or implied question. It is truly amazing how many salesmen, skillful in handling all other segments of the sale, fail to recognize this and never ask for the order. One almost gets the impression that they view selling as a game to be played not for winning but for the game's sake. That type of thinking wins Boy Scout merit badges, not sales. If we know that the product we are selling fills the need and that the value is present, there is absolutely nothing wrong in pressing as hard as good taste will allow for the close. Too many salesmen are victims of their trade's movie, television, and book publicity, which paints them as brassy or "pushy" types who get strangleholds on prospects, and do not let up until the innocent customer cries, "Uncle! I'll sign!" What a pity that some of us feel compelled to go to the opposite extreme just to prove how wrong this image is.

Another reason for the failure of some to ask The Question is something we covered earlier—anxiety. Appreciating the importance of the customer's final answer, and worrying about it to the extent that we train to make him say "yes" as often as possible, is one thing. However, when we stop to think about what happens if he says no, and we are uncertain of where to go from there, anxiety sets in. Our mouths become dry, our palms or foreheads are bathed in perspiration, and we take the "safer" route of not even asking for the order. What a waste of energy! Customers don't bite, and there is simply no other way to build sales volume.

So much has been written about closings that it is inconceivable that there is a salesman working who does not know that they are an integral part of the sale. Yet this, too, is sometimes the case. In most of these instances the salesman and/or his trainer have actually fallen in love with their product. Steeped in product knowledge, they just know that it is good and worth the price. All of this is important, of course, but where does the payoff for all of this training come in? Obviously, we know that the payoff is in the close, but the customer does not know it. Furthermore, we must never forget that few of us are blessed with selling a product that is an absolute necessity. The prospect may want what we have, but he can just as easily want something else, unless we bolster his confidence by guiding him to the close.

This business of closing is really not so difficult. In fact, in one way or another it is as simple as ABC. Or, to put it another way, the salesman's true job is to Always Be Closing. If we remember that, no matter how imperfect our form, we will never forget to ask for the order. *Always Be Closing*—for several reasons, we should do exactly that from the moment we first encounter a prospect. Time is one of the seller's most important assets. There are just so many hours in a day, and a limited number of customers who can be seen during that period. Even if they all bought, there would still be a difference of results on the sales floor, with the star performer being the one who saw the most prospects. That is one reason why sales should be concluded as quickly as possible. Another is the fact that some salesmen have actually talked themselves out of a sale by failing to close soon enough. The more they speak, the more familiar the customer becomes with them and their product. While this is fine, up to a point, it is foolish to risk exposing negative personality traits or product features that may have no bearing on the effectiveness of the item, but that can give the prospect second thoughts and open up new objections.

If we are, therefore, always closing, the form of the close should vary from one situation to the next. A retail candy salesman, for example, cannot spend much time in planning strategy. There is not enough profit in the product to compensate him for spending more than a moment or two with each customer. Also, with impulse purchases of this sort, the customer has usually qualified himself by asking for a specific brand. All that remains for the salesman to do is close the sale by putting the package on the counter and requesting payment. It sounds so simple, and it is effective, but the salesman who sells a more expensive item had better not try it. The customer who spends a larger amount of money expects and is entitled to receive more attention from the salesman. He would be justifiably wary of an obvious attempt to close the moment he walked into the store. *Always Be Closing*, in this case, means always point toward the close.

If he is fortunate, the salesman may be able to lead his prospect to what has been called an "automatic" close. In this procedure the seller takes the buyer, logically, through each step of the sale, until all the needs have been established and the customer agrees that the product fills those needs. In a somewhat abbreviated form, the conversation on the sales floor might go something like this:

"Good morning. How may we serve you?"

"I'd like to see a new model gizmo."

"Yes, sir. It is available in two colors. This is the latest fashion red, and this is the more quiet green. Were you planning to buy it for yourself or for a gift?"

"For myself."

"Well, then, what is the color of your kitchen cabinets?"

"Brown."

"In that case, I would suggest the green. The colors are so handsomely complementary. Will you take it with you, or shall we deliver it?"

A story-book sale, you say? Not necessarily so. Of course, there may be questions from the customer in between those statements, but only if they are very important to him. Notice how the salesman remained in control throughout the transaction, keeping the conversation going his way, and how it was unnecessary for the customer to say, "I'll take it," before the salesman went into his close. Oh, you missed it. Well, the innocuous question about delivery was the close. From that point on, there was nothing for the salesman to do but learn how payment would be made (cash or charge), thank the customer, and move on to the next prospect. There is no point to making more of it than that!

"But what does one do," you might ask, "if the customer balks? Suppose right down at the wire he says that he has not quite decided to buy yet, and talk of delivery is premature?"

Well, no harm has been done. Heading toward the "automatic" close, we are at least able to smoke out objections that the prospect may have, but that we cannot overcome until he voices them. If he does say that he will "be back," we can always remind him that our sale is ending today, tell him about our free trial offer or the store's policy of guaranteed satisfaction. The point is that an attempted close, even an unsuccessful one, is an important and valuable sales tool.

However, make no mistake about it. There is nothing

automatic about even an "automatic" close. A salesman must work as hard at this end of the sale as he does at the beginning. At this point, all of those fears we mentioned in earlier chapters come to a head. More often than not it is a subconscious realization, but the customer senses that he has reached the point of no return. Usually, once the merchandise or service is bought, there is no opportunity to change his mind, at least not without considerable fuss and bother. Is there something wrong with the product that the salesman skillfully avoided mentioning? Once he takes possession, will it continue to appear so attractive? After the sale is made, will the company lose interest in him and leave him to fend for himself in such matters as product service? And, if he shopped just a little longer, could he buy the same item for less elsewhere? These are questions that, in varying degrees, are going through the prospect's mind even after the sale is consummated.

The close is the last chance the salesman has to put his customer at ease, and, if the product is to remain sold, we must do just that. Also, let us not forget the cumulative value of what the customer tells his friends about how well he was treated and the satisfaction he received. Therefore, although the prospect may have said yes, it may be advisable to volunteer the services of a home demonstrator to follow up the delivery truck.

Some salesmen deliberately break contact with the customer after the sale. "When you call to make certain that everything is all right," they say, "it is an invitation to the customer to find fault. He will mention things he never would have bothered to call about on his own." Talk about a shortsighted lack of confidence! With so little faith in a product, those salesmen have no business selling it.

Fortunately, the majority of us have assurance in ourselves, our product, and our customers. We approach the close and the post-close confidently. All that remains is to impart this same feeling, through a smooth close, to the prospect.

Pressing for a yes or no answer is, generally, not the best way to allay those fears. On the contrary, it make evoke the very "trapped" feeling we wish to avoid. It is better by far for the customer to decide whether he wants this or that color, delivery today or tomorrow, or make some other decision that does not have the ring of finality that saying yes to the purchase has.

Return to our example of a few pages ago, and observe how our closing question gave the prospect a choice between taking the item with him or having it delivered. No yes or no nonsense here. Such questions, which the reader will surely recognize as being open-ended, are the basis for all good closes. Those you employ will naturally depend upon what you are selling, but, if you stay away from any hint of, "Well, do you or do you not want it?" you will have no trouble.

Knowing just when to go into the close should also not be too difficult. Oddly enough, it is the customer himself who usually tells us when the time is ripe. The sad part about all of this, though, is that the salesman is sometimes so busy leading up to the point at which he thinks the close should be that he fails to recognize the fact that the customer is there before him. For instance, what do all of these prospect comments and questions have in common?

"That one looks nice."

"Can you deliver tonight?"

"I'd prefer the smaller size."

"Sounds reasonable."

"Can I pay for it in installments?"

"Which would you recommend?"

All of those are closing *signals* that the prospect might give the salesman. There is absolutely no way of knowing when they will occur, because the "trigger" for each customer is different. Sometimes you will have to listen very carefully to hear them. They may even take the form of an approving nod of the head, which you can easily miss if you are not looking for it. When you do catch the signal, no matter how or when it is thrown, there is just one thing to do—drop the remainder of your prepared talk and ask an open-ended question calculated to close the sale then and there.

Of course, there are times when that buying signal never seems to come. The customer appears to be willing to let the salesman talk, talk, and talk. Eagerly, we look for the "go ahead and write up the order" sign, but it is not there. If we simply continue to the end without any interruption, we might just as well hand the prospect a recording and let him get the sales message from that. Furthermore, there is nothing quite so boring as a salesman who has said all there is to say about his product, and who is left with only the choice of repeating himself or launching into an abrupt close. No, somewhere along the line we must stimulate the prospect or else interrupt ourselves.

"Do you prefer this new method of washing clothes or your old one?" the home laundry salesman can ask.

"The black is good for evening wear, and the blue is perfect for afternoons. When do you intend to wear it?" the dress saleslady might inquire.

And the industrial salesman can ask his prospect, "Would you want to lease this or buy it outright?"

Once again the open-ended question comes to the rescue. There is certainly no rule to guide you when to use it, but when you do, make certain that you employ it while you still have a choice, and not in desperation because you are all talked out.

Just about the most frustrating prospect to sell is the one who gives us no sign of his interest—or even lack of interest. He just sits or stands there while we go through our entire sales talk, resisting every one of our attempts to get him into the act. We met this strong, silent type at qualifying time, and we will surely recognize him when it comes to the close, but how to meet him and keep our "cool" is another matter. Indeed, when all is said and done, there are only two ways to get this sales prospect headed in the right direction.

We can, first of all, make every effort to outwait this fellow. At first it may require summoning a little more nerve than you normally have, but the results of simply standing there, with a pleasant smile on your face and not saying a single word, can be most startling. After what may initially seem like an eternity to you, the prospect will say something. He must, unless he is a hopeless psychotic, and that "something" will probably be quite pleasant. Of course, the gambit to which we are referring is to be tried only in those instances where all other techniques to get the customer talking have been attempted and have failed. There is nothing more to do, then, than play the prospect's game. Even if he says, "Goodbye," we are better off than before, because this gives us the opportunity to start qualifying him all over again by asking his name, etc. "It has been nice chatting with you, Mr. . . . Mr. . . ." we can deliberately fumble. "You know, I didn't catch your name."

A second method for handling the admittedly desperate situation of the prospect who won't talk is to violate our sacred rule about open-ended questions. Remember, we did say that all else had failed! "Well," we might casually mention, "I'm so glad you agree that this model is perfect for your needs. I'll have one delivered tomorrow." Then shift to the silent treatment yourself, and wait. Of course, the prospect never did say that he agreed, but here is his chance to point that out either by raising an objection or giving us an alternative. He must make the next move, and we should be prepared to wait him out.

The reader can appreciate the fact that no book, no matter how long, can hope to provide an answer to every closing situation a salesman will encounter. Customers are always dreaming up new objections and ways to resist a close. Salesmen, being somewhat more adventurous than office workers, are constantly devising different approaches to their job. Some of these are ingeniously successful. Others lead to problems we could never anticipate. For all of these reasons, any discussion of the close would be incomplete without a word to the salesman who has followed the script to the letter, from greeting to closing attempts, but just can't seem to get the customer to say yes.

When all else fails, there is but one thing to do—ask the prospect why you failed. Don't be afraid. Say something such as: "Sir, it has been a pleasure attempting to serve you. I'm sorry that we could not get together on this. However, I wonder if you would mind telling me why you believe this model will not make you happy." We have left ourselves a perfect "out" with this sort of close—if we can call it that—because we referred to the "model" rather than the "product." If we do get an objection that we cannot meet, we can always make one last attempt to shift to another model that seems to more neatly fit the bill. The worst we may learn is some objection we can prepare to overcome before we embark upon our next attempt to close.

Talking and listening—those are the successful salesman's stock in trade. The intelligent application of both can melt any prospect's heart, and lay bare more worlds to conquer than you ever dreamed possible.

Summary

One Hundred Reasons Why Sales Are Lost

Preparing for the sale:

1. Insufficient product knowledge of salesman
2. Uninviting displays
3. No point-of-purchase sales material
4. Failure of salesman to meet prospect
5. Salesman's lack of confidence
6. Salesman's physical or emotional illness
7. Salesman's sloppy personal appearance
8. Overcrowded sales floor
9. Demonstrator models not operating
10. "Sell" model too close to the door
11. Too many salesmen
12. Uncomfortable physical atmosphere

Greeting the prospect:

13. Forgetting to call the customer by name
14. Waiting for the prospect to greet him

15. Using a closed-end greeting
16. No salesman in sight
17. Failure to establish empathy
18. Forgetting to smile
19. Lack of enthusiasm
20. Greeting more than one prospect at once
21. Not looking at the customer
22. Being busy with something else during the greeting
23. Using slang
24. Setting a time limit
25. Shouting
26. Answering "no" to the prospect's first question

Getting into the sale:

27. Not listening
28. Failing to hear prospect's "wants"
29. Lack of comfortable sales atmosphere
30. Inability to get prospect's complete attention
31. Uncertainty of what we want to sell
32. Jumping too quickly to an obvious close
33. Not establishing prospect's "needs"
34. Failure to make customer want what he needs
35. Not taking into account fears present in the sale
36. Commencing with price
37. Leaping to conclusions
38. Forgetting to "sell" ourselves
39. Ignoring an old complaint
40. Failing to hold the customer's attention
41. Being argumentative
42. Reacting to emotionally laden words
43. Not having advertised product available
44. Deprecating competition

45. Using emotionally laden words
46. Attempting to serve more than one customer at once
47. Downgrading our "promotional leader"
48. Failing to establish initial basis for agreement
49. Admitting failure too easily
50. Inviting bargaining on price

At demonstration time:

51. Imperfect working models
52. Demonstrating in a strange environment
53. Stepping too quickly to higher-priced units
54. Fumbling with controls
55. Failure to invite prospect to "try it" himself
56. Making excuses for the product
57. Asking for assistance
58. Leaving the demonstration to answer a phone call
59. Using too much flattery
60. Failing to make appointment with the prospect
61. Insulting the customer's intelligence
62. Scaring the prospect
63. Offering no after-sale assistance
64. Inability to answer technical questions
65. Offering a "free" home trial with strings attached
66. Bragging
67. Getting too technical
68. Dirtying the prospect's floor
69. Lying
70. Demonstrating the wrong product

Meeting objections:

71. Losing our temper

72. Failing to agree
73. Ignoring objections
74. Not realizing the true basis for the objection
75. Providing unbelievable answers
76. Talking too much
77. Making light of objections
78. Not having an answer
79. Failing to press for a close after objection was met
80. Answering objections that were not raised
81. Failing to turn objection into a customer benefit
82. Implying prospect ignorance
83. Returning to the objection after it has been met
84. Hesitating
85. Being sidetracked by an objection

At the close:

86. Not asking for the order
87. Failing to recognize a buying signal
88. Asking a closed-end question
89. Requesting assistance in writing up the order
90. Attempting to close before the customer is sold
91. Failure to spark prospect's want for the product
92. Repeating the sales message
93. Falling in love with the sound of our own voice
94. Lack of confidence in the product
95. Attempting to "slip in" something we haven't mentioned
96. Ignoring after-sale customer fears
97. Inability to locate customer's "trigger" for closing
98. Poor choice in open-end question
99. Settling for first refusal
100. Being afraid